INSTANT Piano Songs

Audio Access Included

KIDS' POP SONGS
Simple Sheet Music + Audio Play-Along

PLAYBACK+
Speed • Pitch • Balance • Loop

T0071618

To access audio visit:
www.halleonard.com/mylibrary
Enter Code
3952-5948-2756-6252

ISBN 978-1-70514-842-6

HAL•LEONARD®

Visit Hal Leonard Online at
www.halleonard.com

Contact us:
Hal Leonard
7777 West Bluemound Road
Milwaukee, WI 53213
Email: info@halleonard.com

In Europe, contact:
Hal Leonard Europe Limited
42 Wigmore Street
Marylebone, London, W1U 2RN
Email: info@halleonardeurope.com

In Australia, contact:
Hal Leonard Australia Pty. Ltd.
4 Lentara Court
Cheltenham, Victoria, 3192 Australia
Email: info@halleonard.com.au

Welcome to the *INSTANT Piano Songs* series!

This unique, flexible collection allows you to play with either one hand or two. Three playing options are available—all of which sound great with the online backing tracks:

1. **Play only the melody with your right hand.**

2. **Add basic chords in your left hand, which are notated for you.**

3. **Use suggested rhythm patterns for the left-hand chords.**

Letter names appear inside the notes in both hands to assist you, and there are no key signatures to worry about. If a **sharp ♯** or **flat ♭** is needed, it is shown beside the note each time, even within the same measure.

If two notes are connected by a **tie** ⌣, hold the first note for the combined number of beats. (The second note does not show a letter name since it is not re-struck.)

Sometimes the melody needs to be played an octave higher to avoid overlapping with the left-hand chords. (If your starting note is C, the next C to the right is one octave higher.) If you are using only your right hand, however, you can disregard this instruction in the music.

🔊 The backing tracks are designed to enhance the piano arrangements, regardless of how you choose to play them. Each track includes two measures of count-off clicks at the beginning. If the recording is too fast or too slow, use the online *PLAYBACK+* player to adjust it to a more comfortable tempo (speed).

Optional left-hand rhythm patterns are provided for when you are ready to move beyond the basic chords. The patterns are based on the three notes of the basic chords and appear as small, gray notes in the first line of each song. Feel free to use the suggested pattern throughout the song, or create your own. Sample rhythm patterns are shown below. (Of course, you can always play just the basic chords if you wish!)

Have fun! Whether you play with one hand or two, you'll sound great!

Sample Rhythm Patterns

4/4 Meter

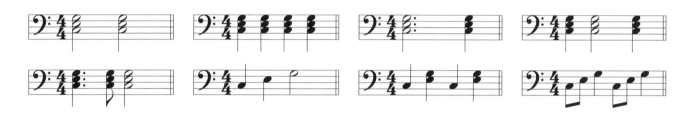

3/4 Meter

6/8 Meter

Also Available

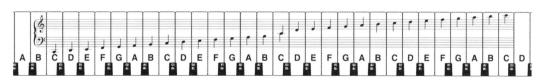

Hal Leonard Student Keyboard Guide HL00296039

Key Stickers HL00100016

Bang!

Words and Music by Adam Metzger,
Jack Metzger and Ryan Metzger

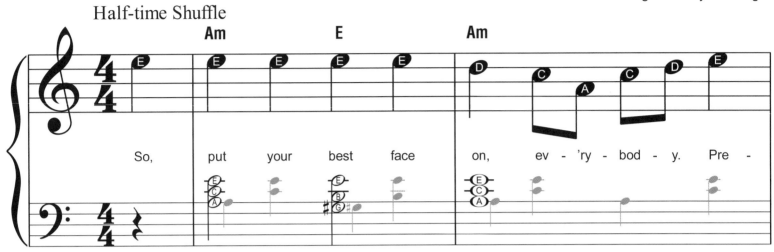

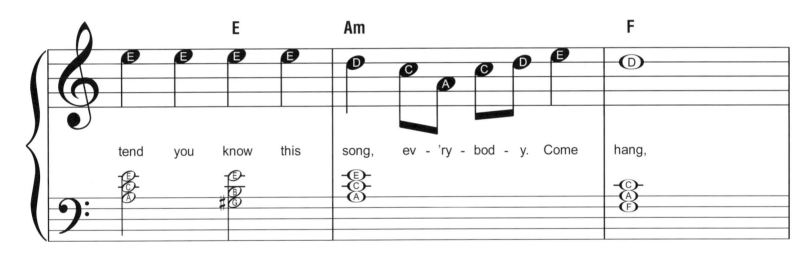

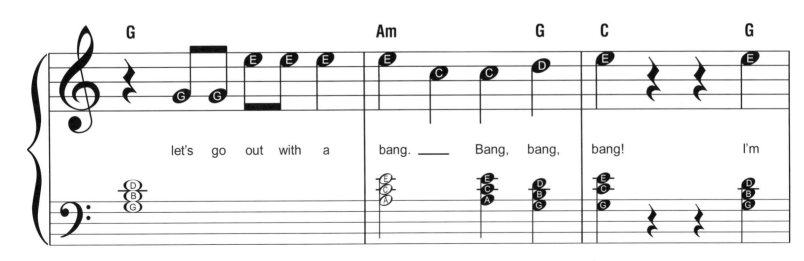

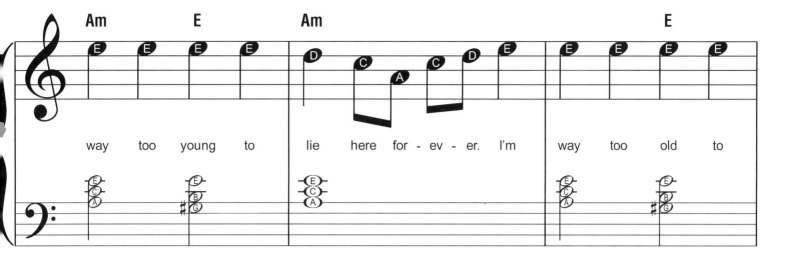

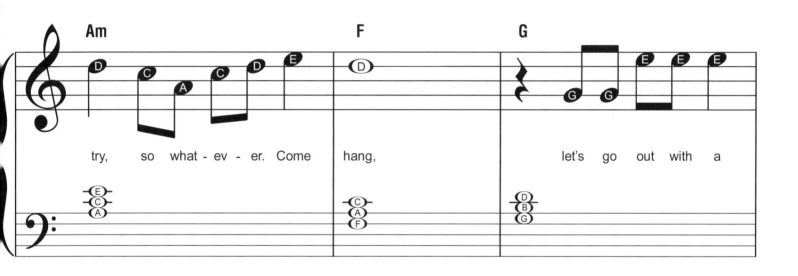

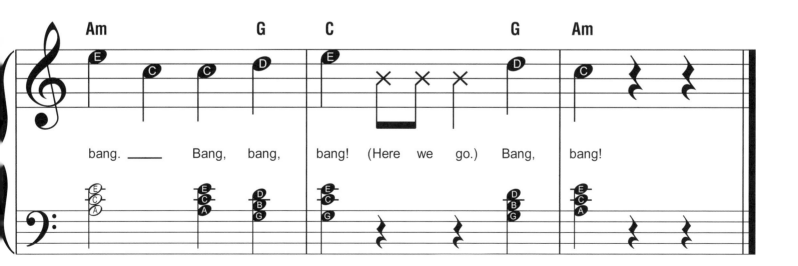

Best Day of My Life

Words and Music by Zachary Barnett,
James Adam Shelley, Matthew Sanchez,
David Rublin, Shep Goodman
and Aaron Accetta

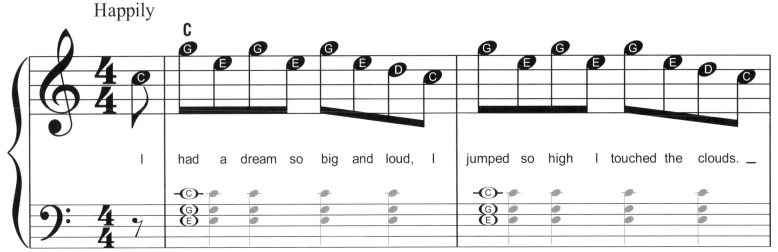

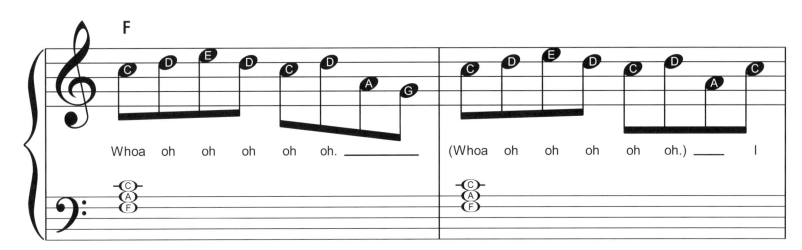

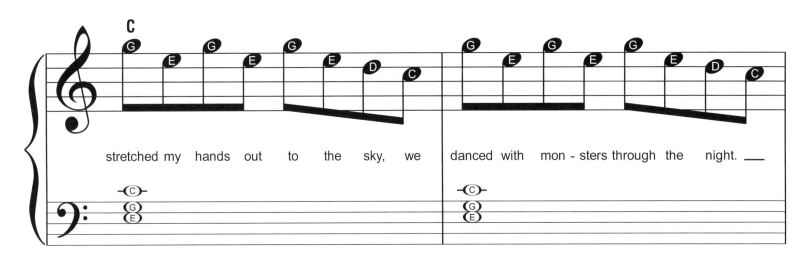

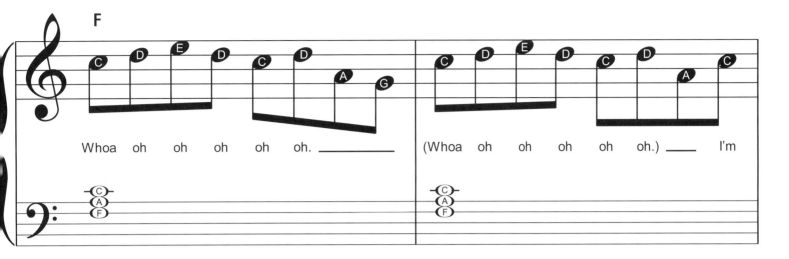

Whoa oh oh oh oh oh. _____ (Whoa oh oh oh oh oh.) _____ I'm

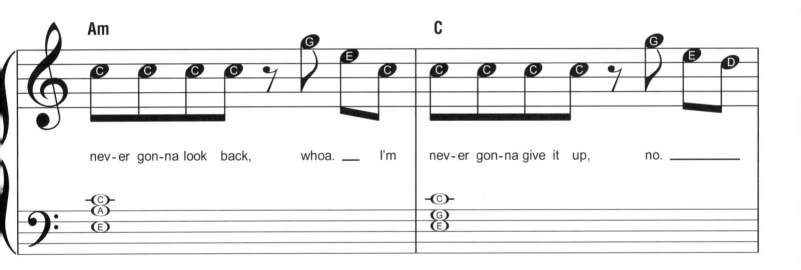

nev-er gon-na look back, whoa. __ I'm nev-er gon-na give it up, no. _____

(no chord)
N.C.

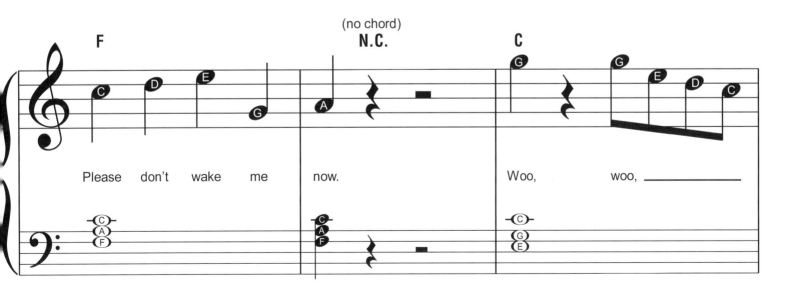

Please don't wake me now. Woo, woo, _____

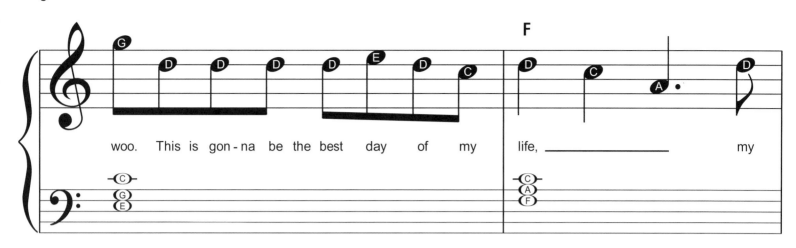

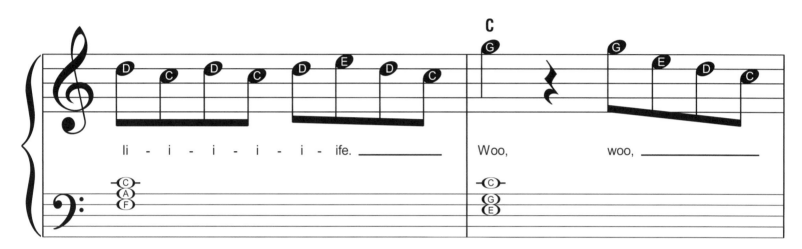

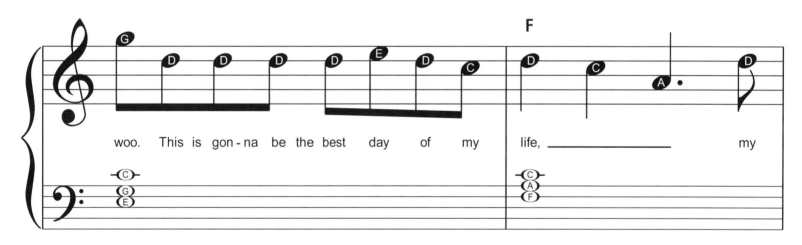

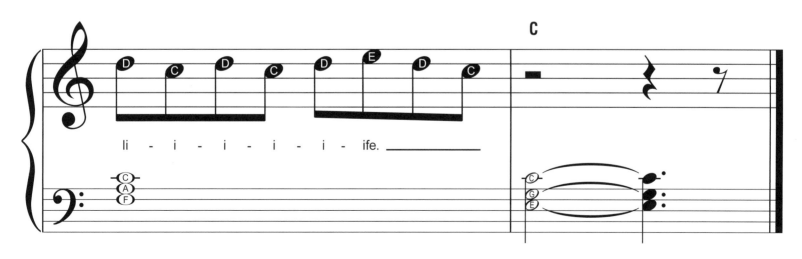

Adore You

Words and Music by Harry Styles,
Thomas Hull, Tyler Johnson
and Amy Allen

Moderate Pop Rock

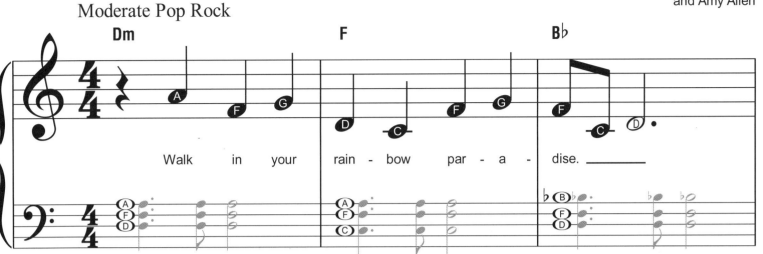

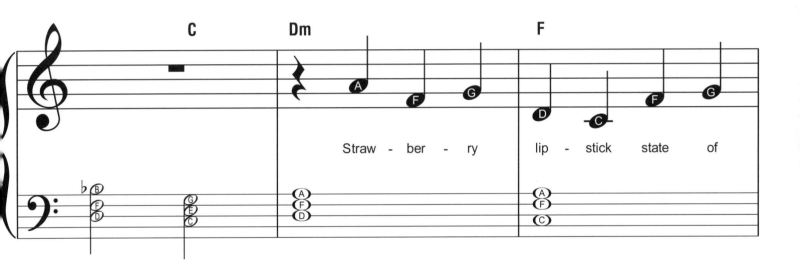

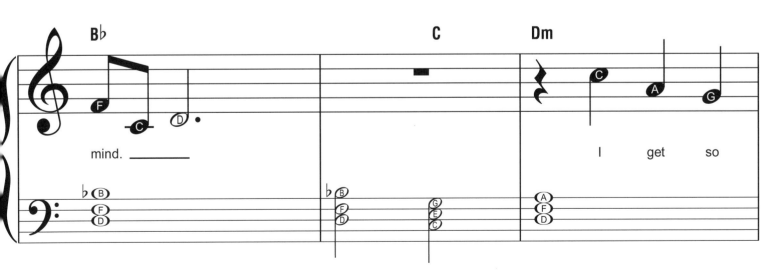

Dance Monkey

Words and Music by
Toni Watson

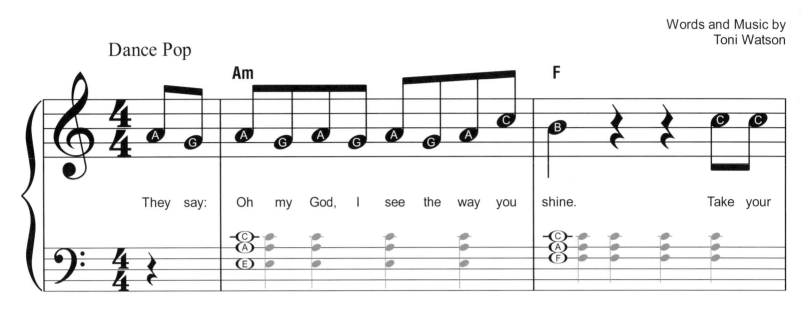

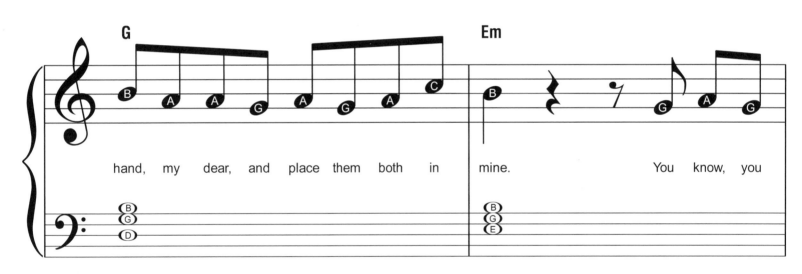

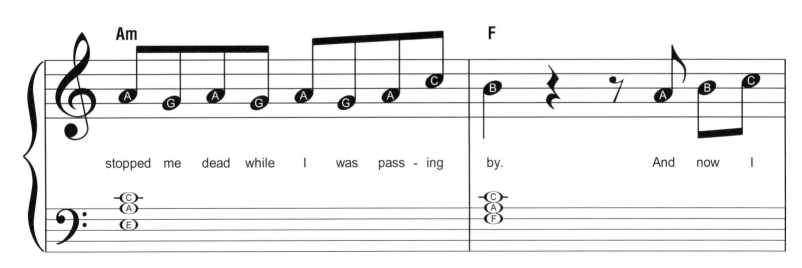

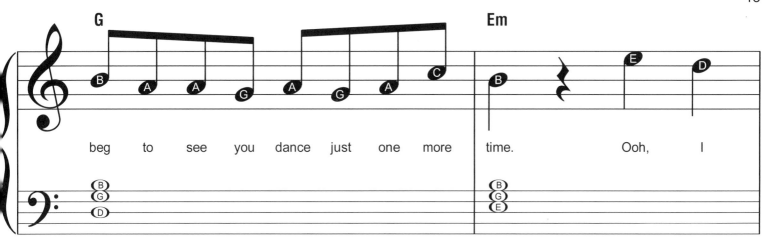

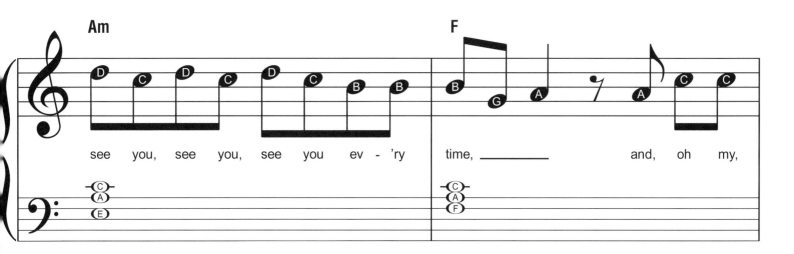

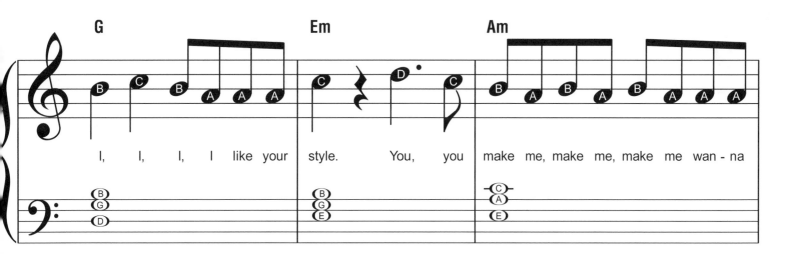

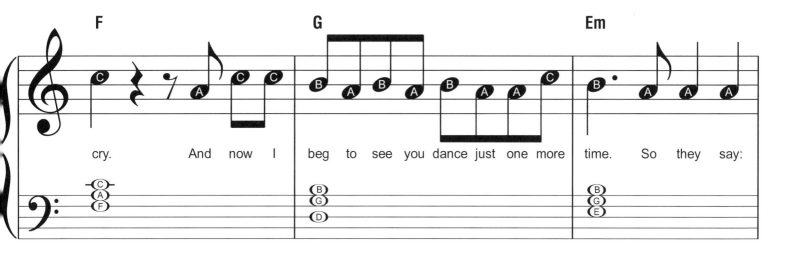

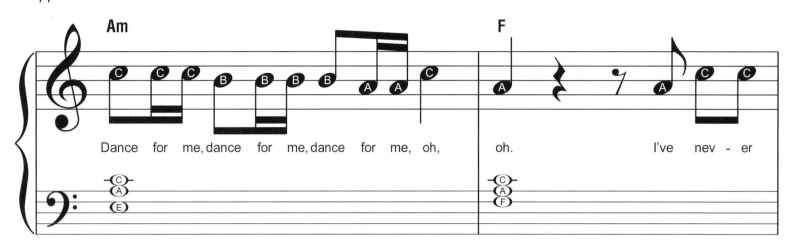

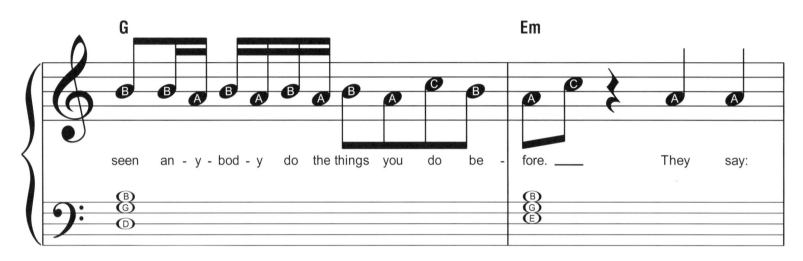

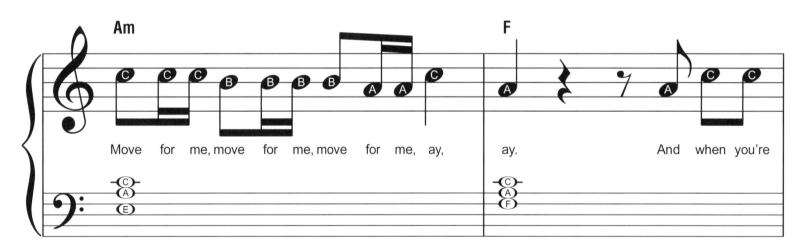

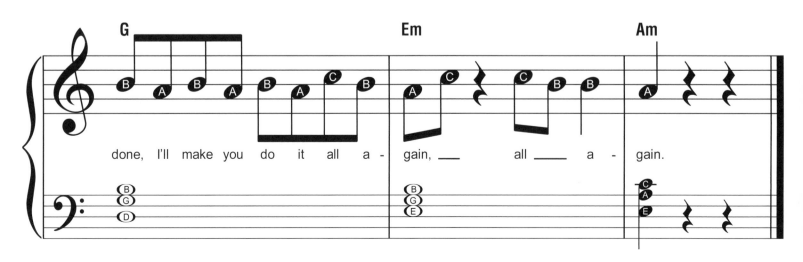

Cool Kids

Words and Music by Graham Sierota,
Jamie Sierota, Noah Sierota,
Sydney Sierota, Jeffrey David Sierota
and Jesiah Dzwonek

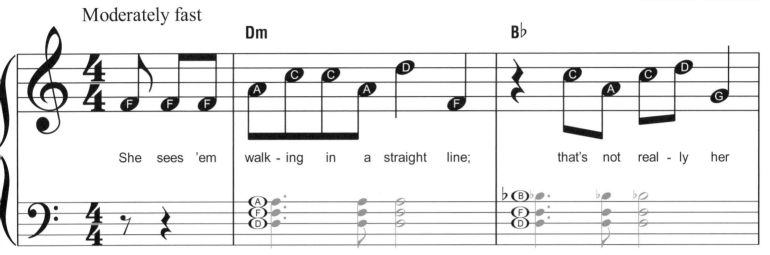

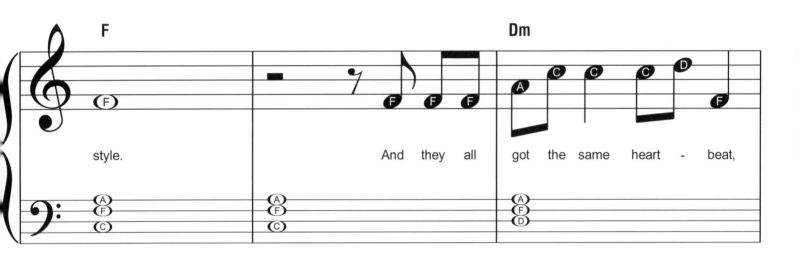

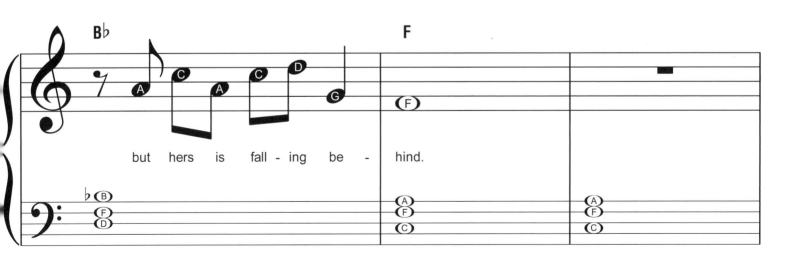

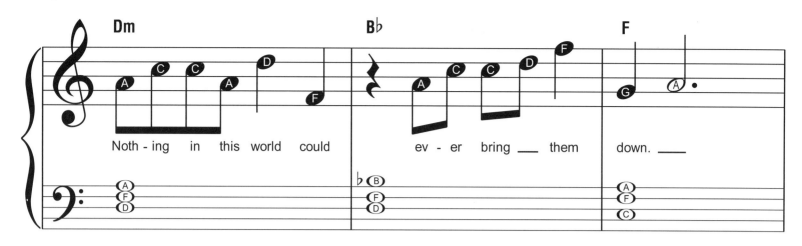

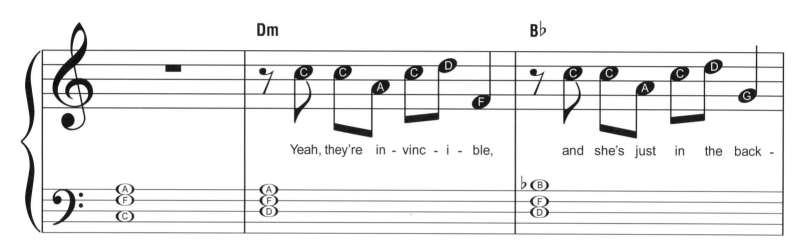

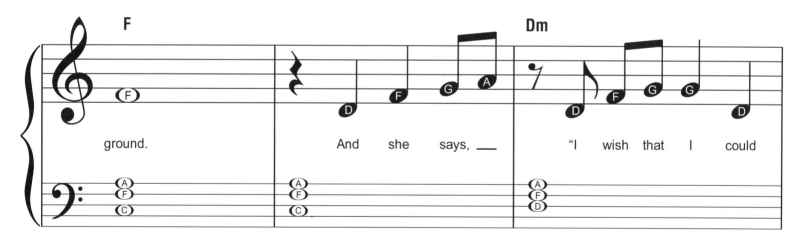

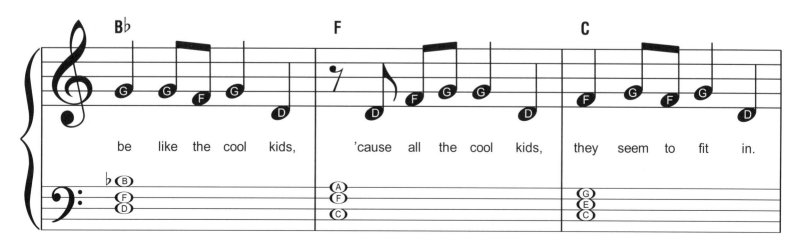

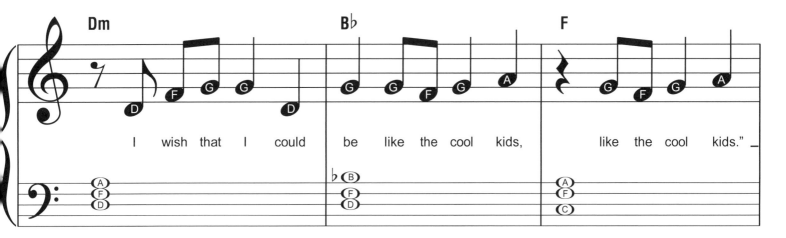

I wish that I could be like the cool kids, like the cool kids."

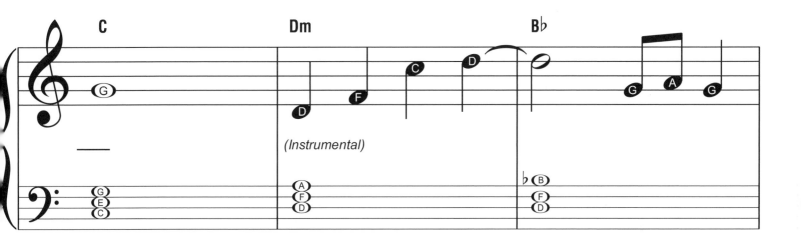

(Instrumental)

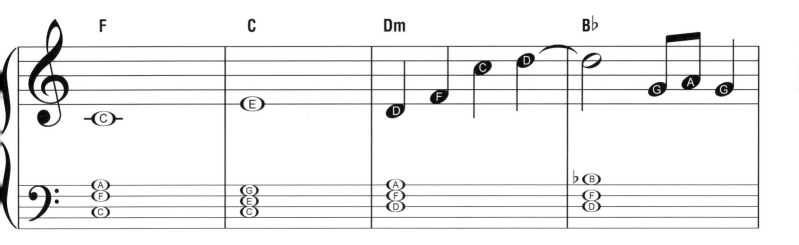

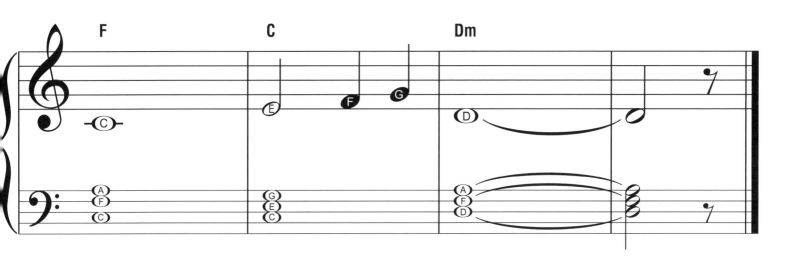

Drivers License

Words and Music by Olivia Rodrigo
and Daniel Nigro

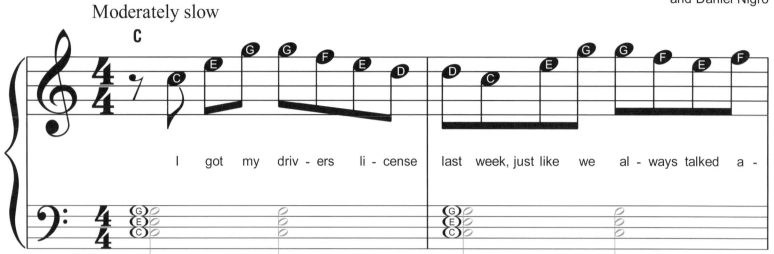

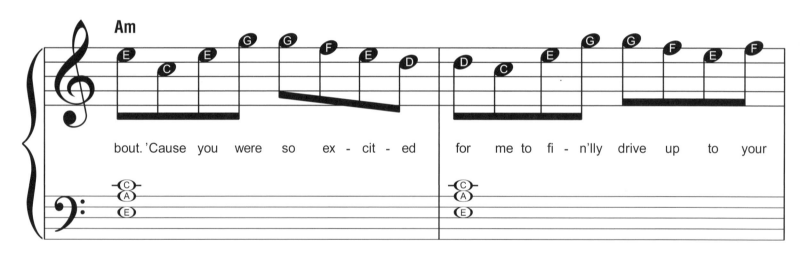

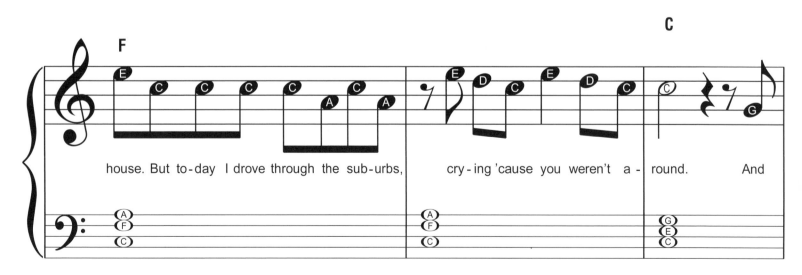

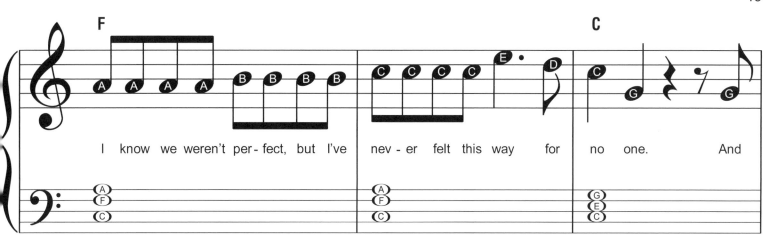

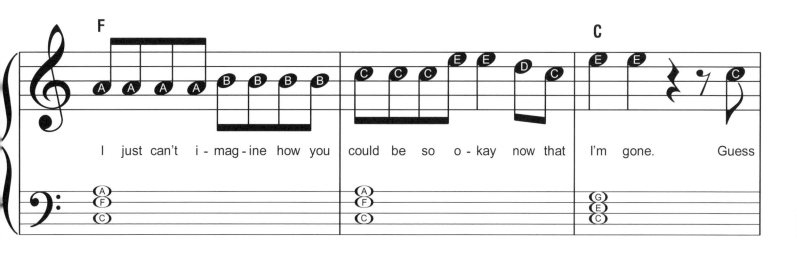

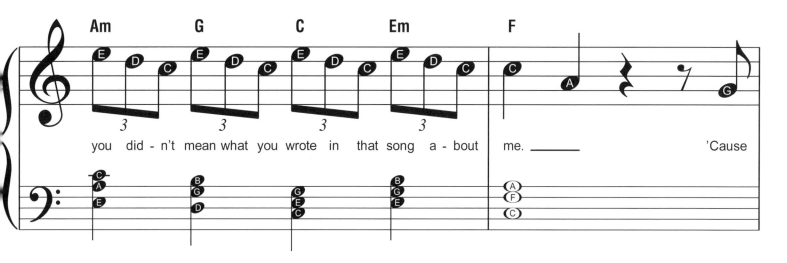

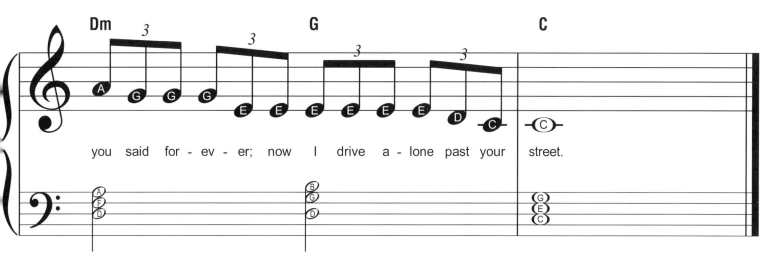

Dynamite

Words and Music by Jessica Agombar
and David Stewart

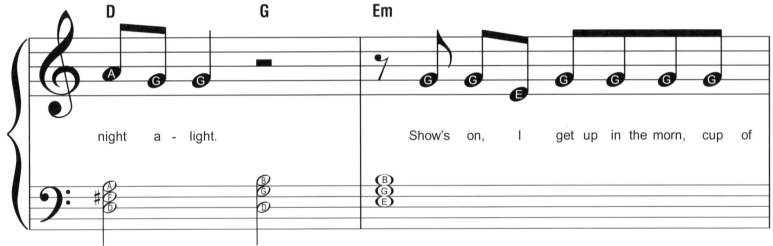

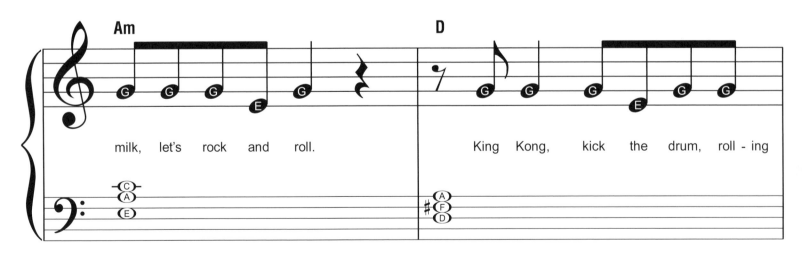

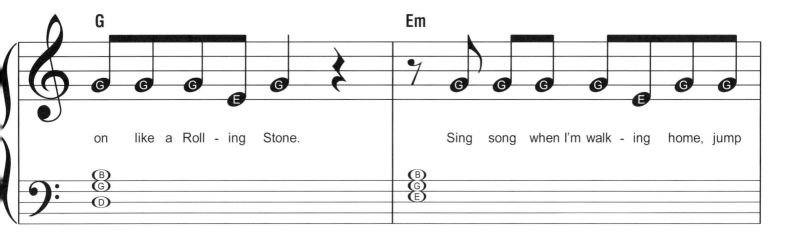

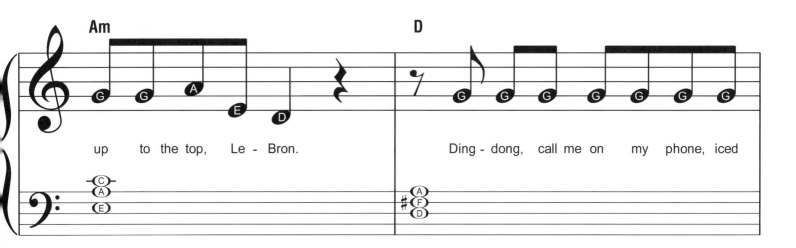

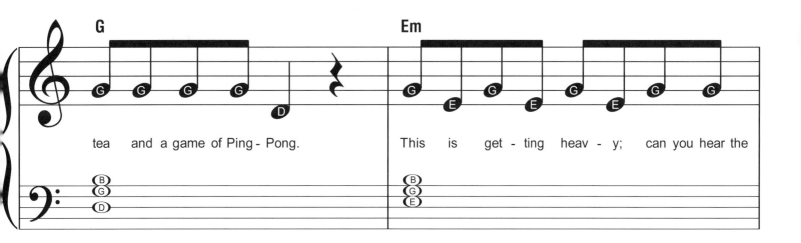

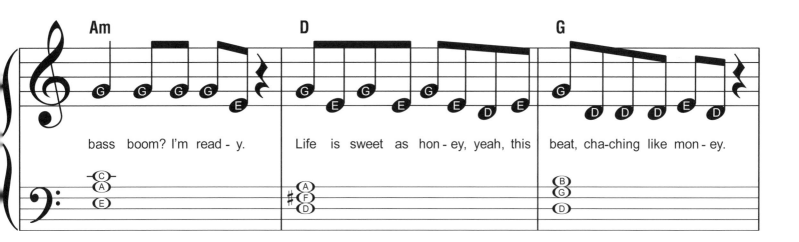

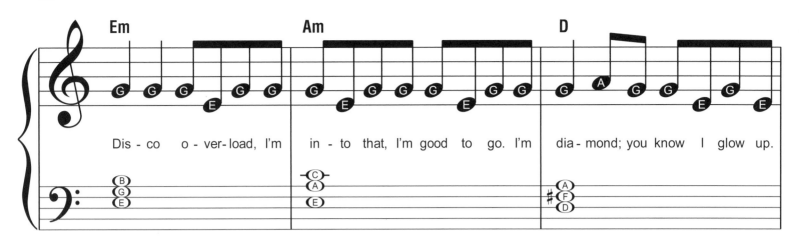

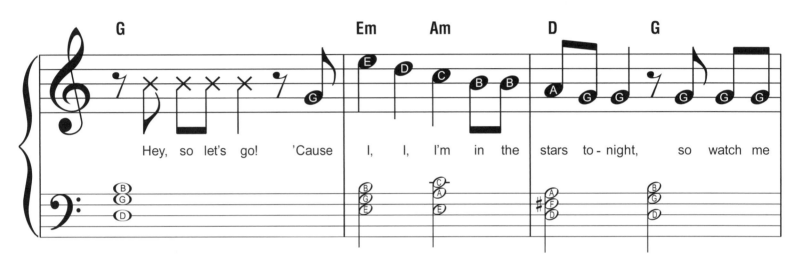

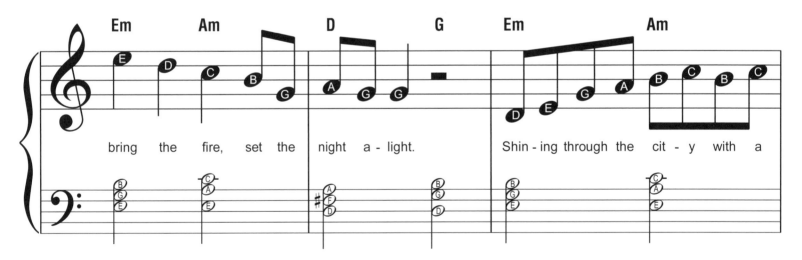

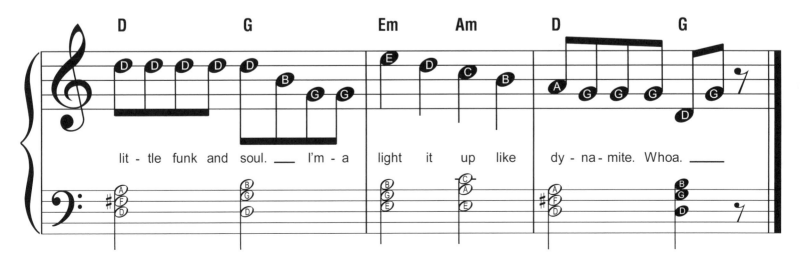

Everything Is Awesome
(Awesome Remixx!!!)
from THE LEGO MOVIE

Words by Shawn Patterson
Music by Andrew Samberg,
Jorma Taccone, Akiva Schaffer,
Joshua Bartholomew, Lisa Harriton
and Shawn Patterson

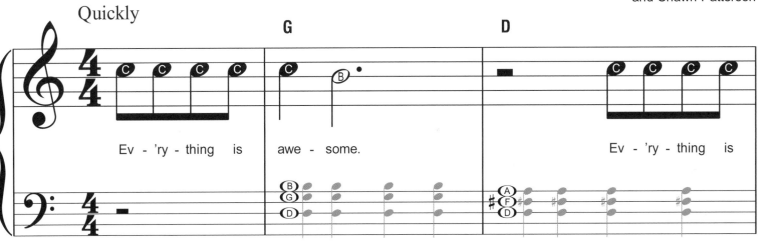

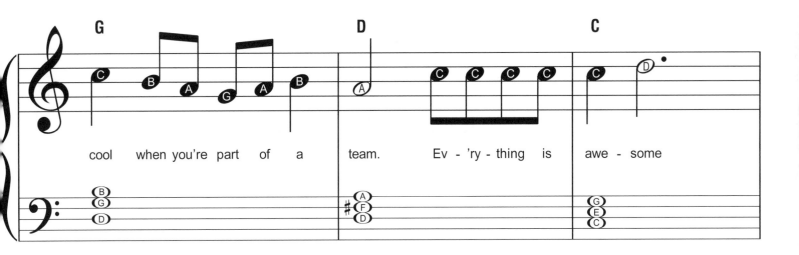

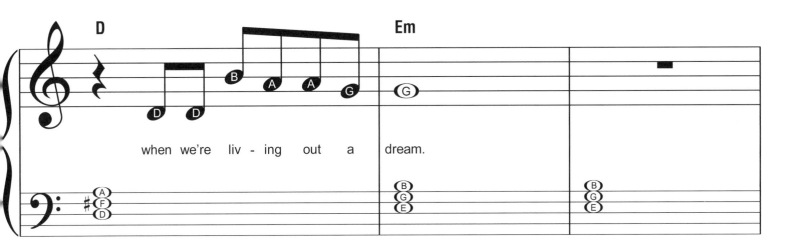

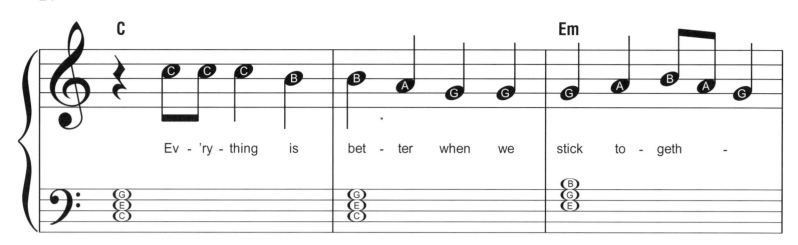

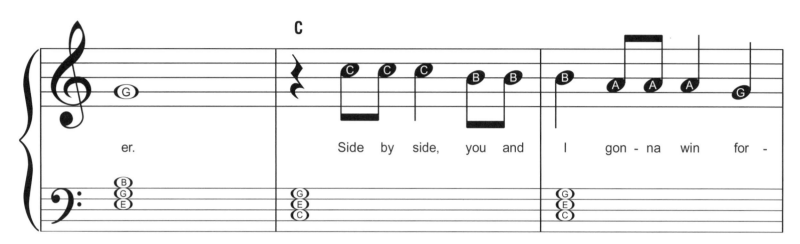

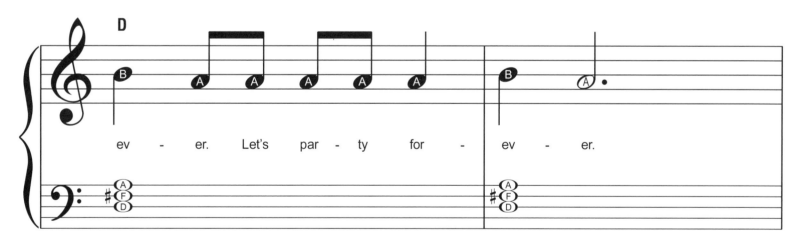

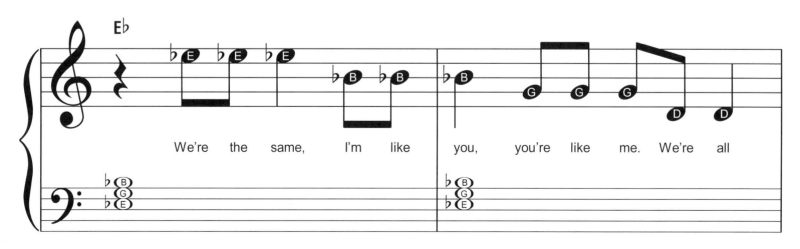

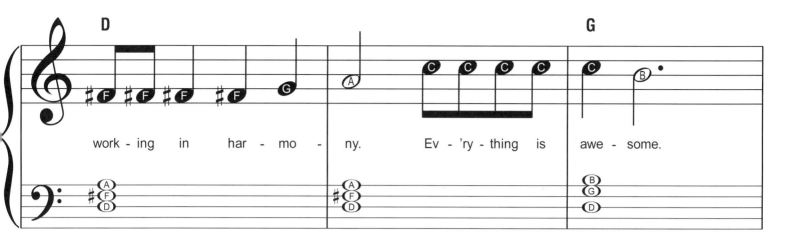

work - ing in har - mo - ny. Ev - 'ry - thing is awe - some.

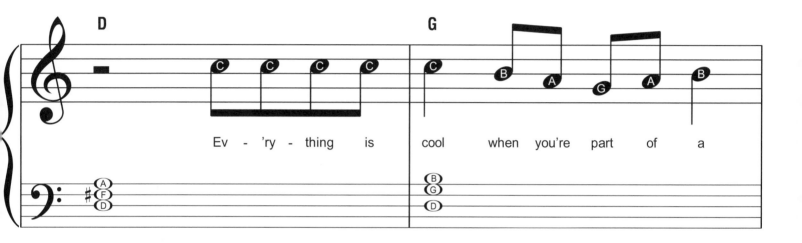

Ev - 'ry - thing is cool when you're part of a

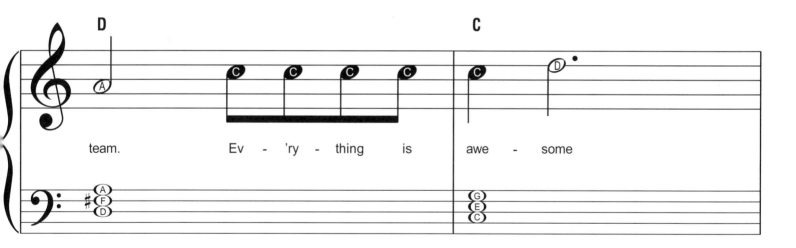

team. Ev - 'ry - thing is awe - some

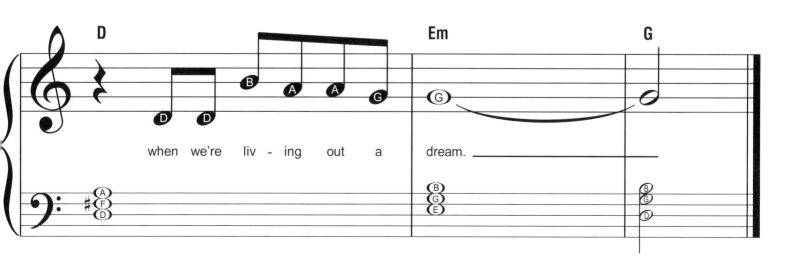

when we're liv - ing out a dream. _____

Fight Song

Words and Music by Rachel Platten
and Dave Bassett

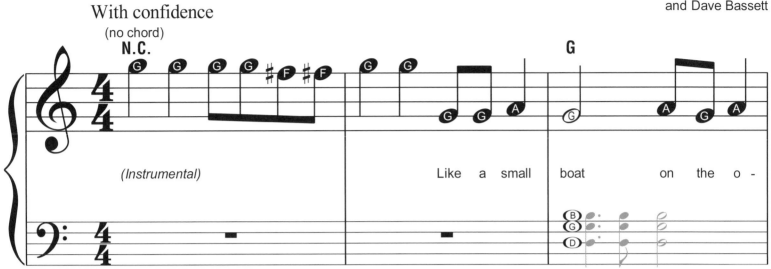

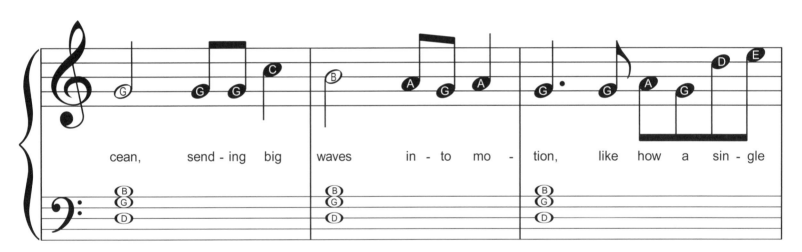

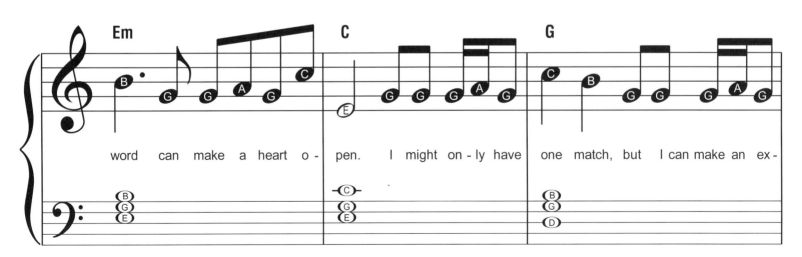

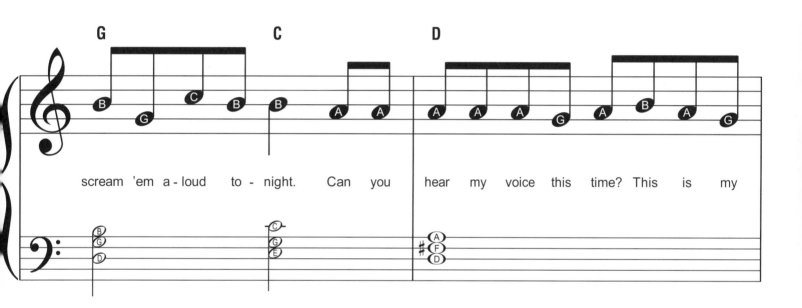

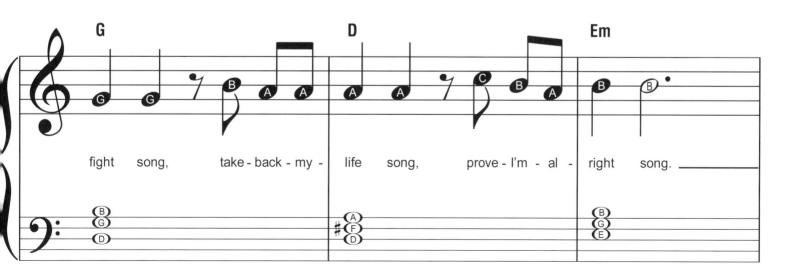

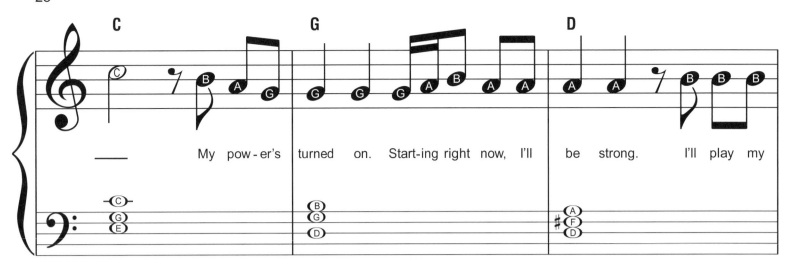

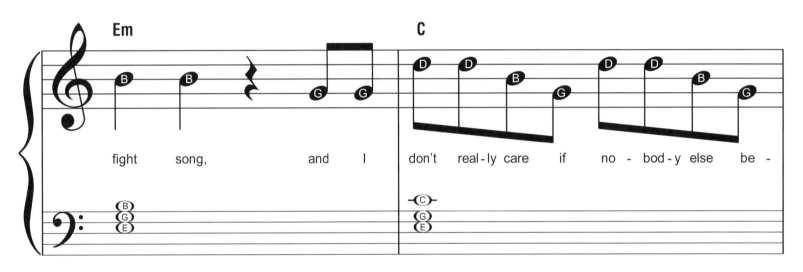

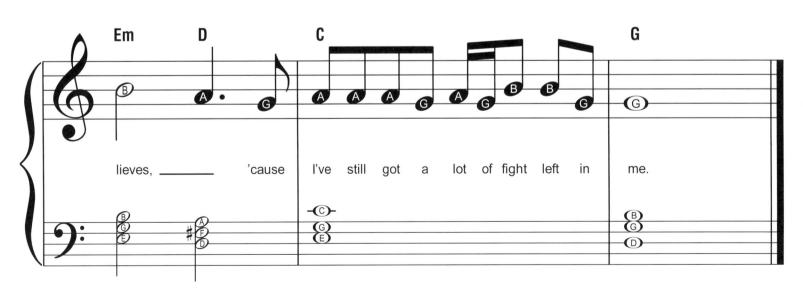

Firework

Words and Music by Katy Perry,
Mikkel Eriksen, Tor Erik Hermansen,
Esther Dean and Sandy Wilhelm

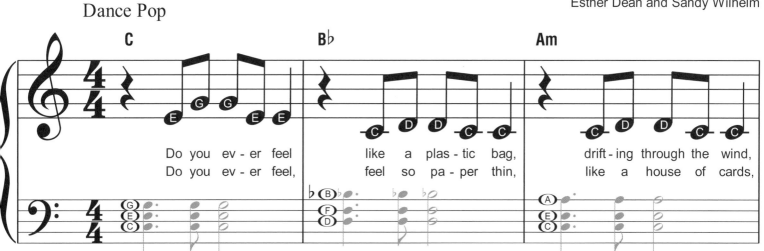

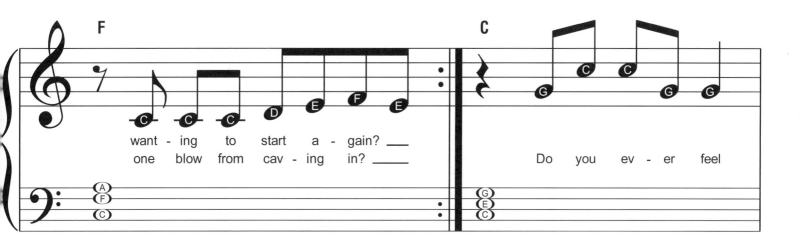

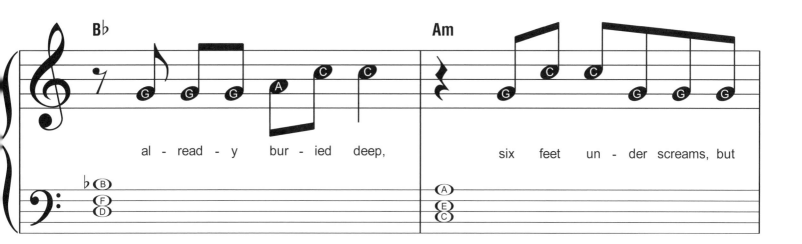

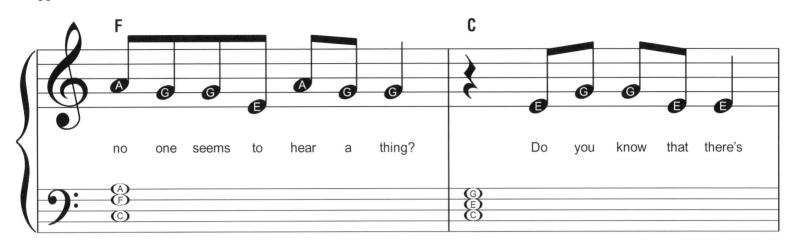

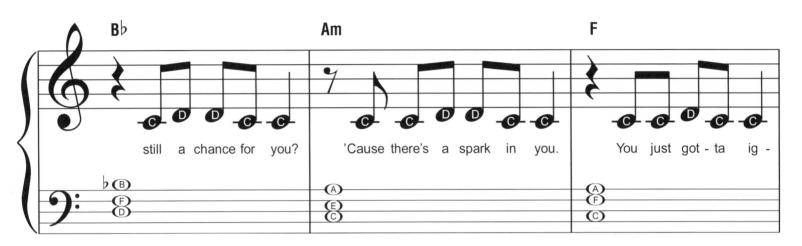

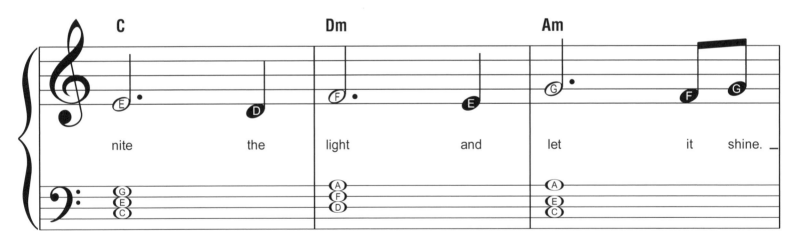

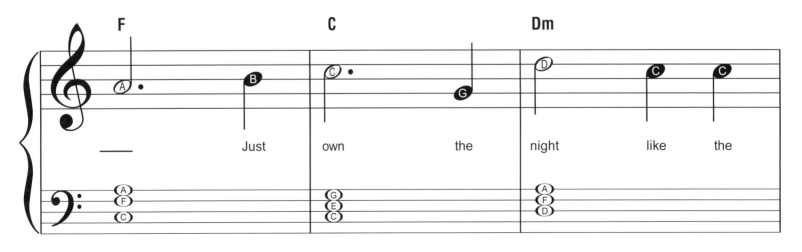

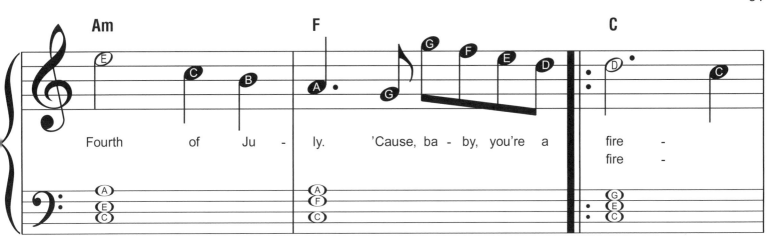

Fourth of Ju - ly. 'Cause, baby, you're a fire -
fire -

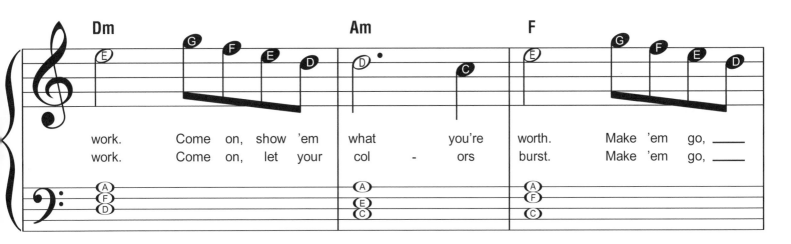

work. Come on, show 'em what you're worth. Make 'em go, _____
work. Come on, let your col - ors burst. Make 'em go, _____

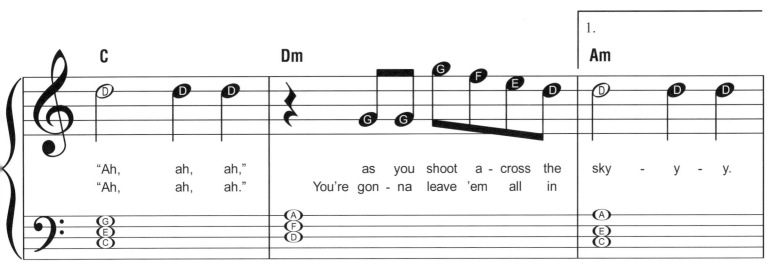

"Ah, ah, ah," as you shoot a - cross the sky - y - y.
"Ah, ah, ah." You're gon - na leave 'em all in

1.

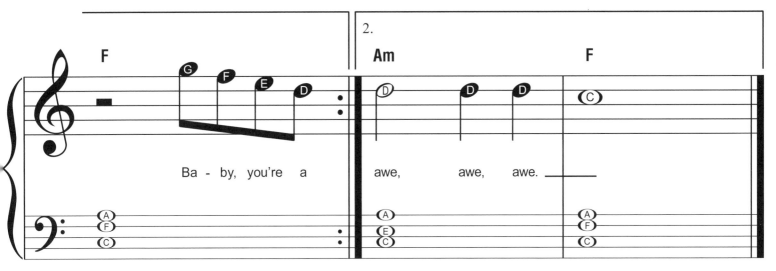

Ba - by, you're a awe, awe, awe. _____

2.

How Far I'll Go

from MOANA

Music and Lyrics by
Lin-Manuel Miranda

Moderately

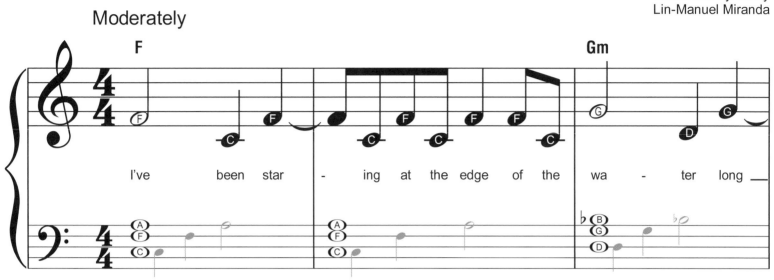

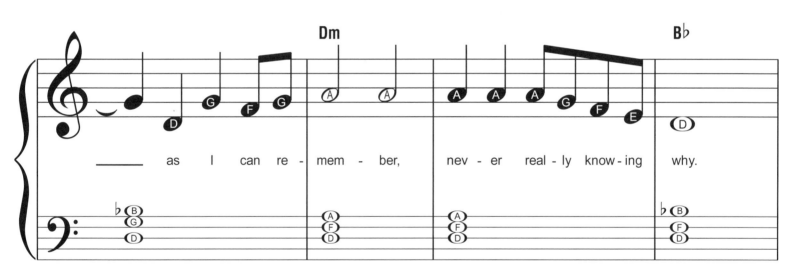

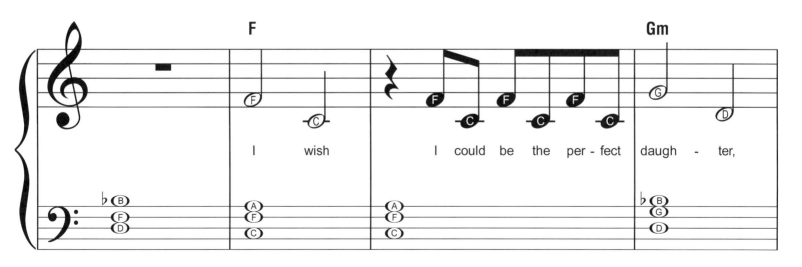

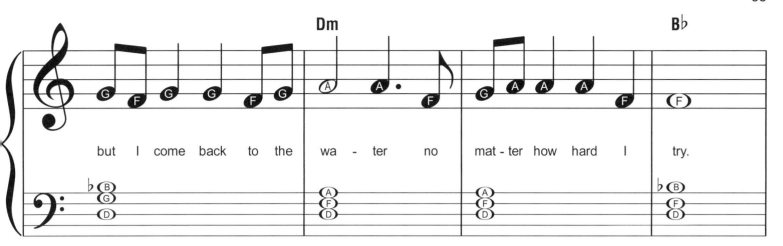

but I come back to the wa - ter no mat - ter how hard I try.

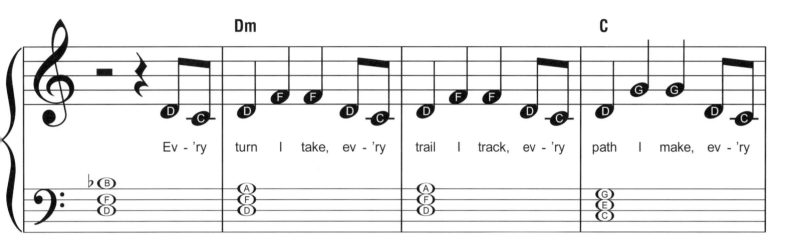

Ev - 'ry turn I take, ev - 'ry trail I track, ev - 'ry path I make, ev - 'ry

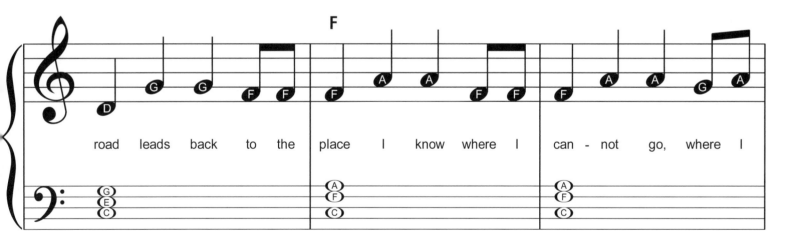

road leads back to the place I know where I can - not go, where I

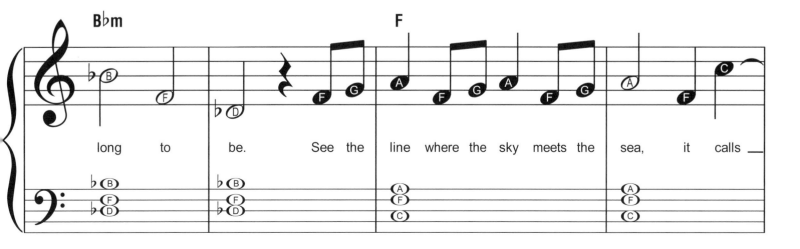

long to be. See the line where the sky meets the sea, it calls ___

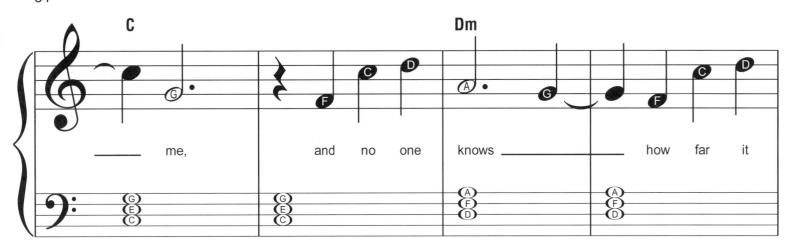

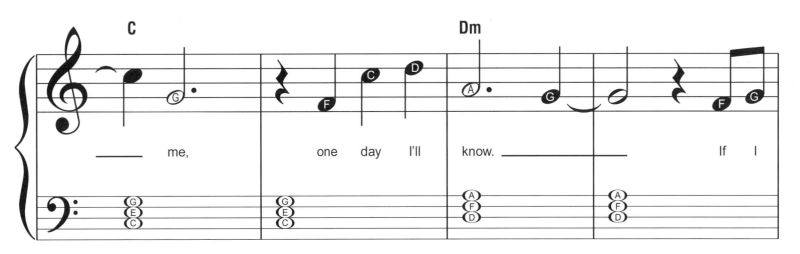

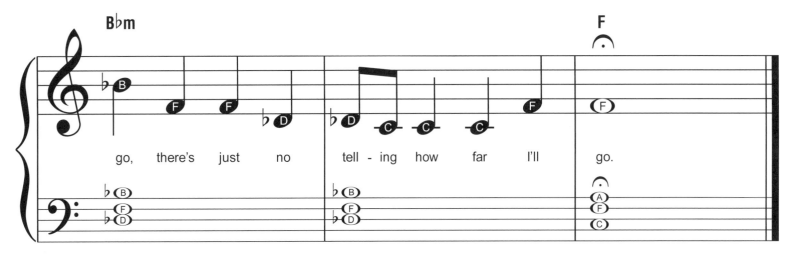

Happy
from DESPICABLE ME 2

Words and Music by
Pharrell Williams

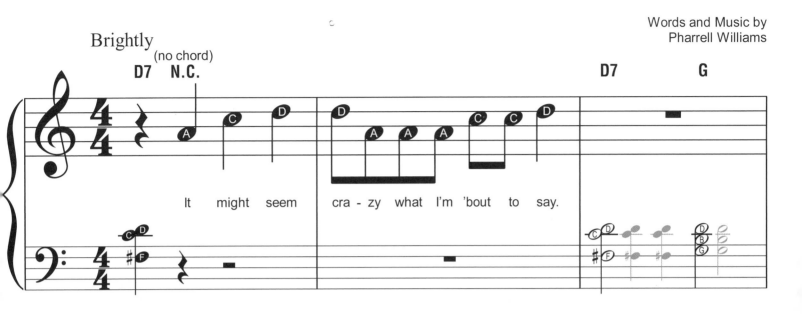

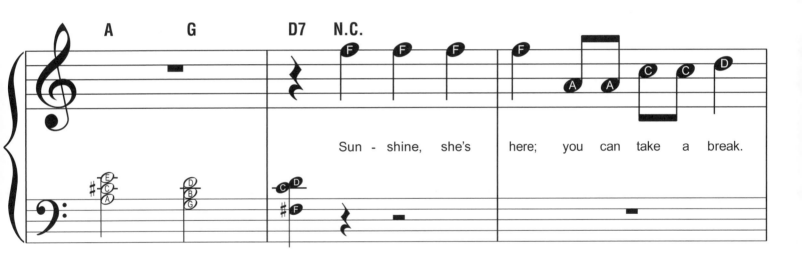

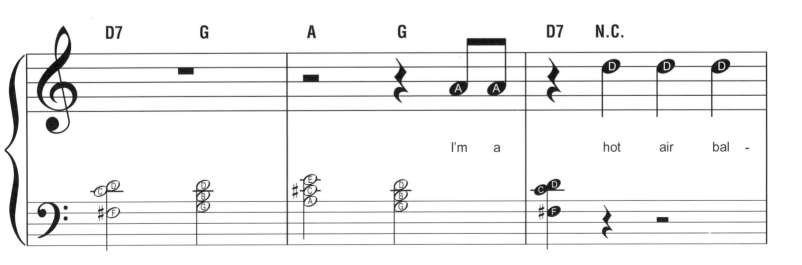

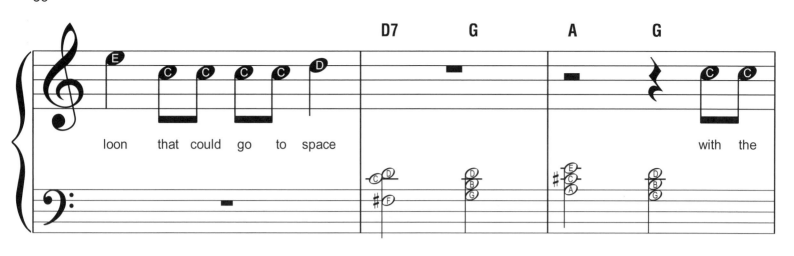

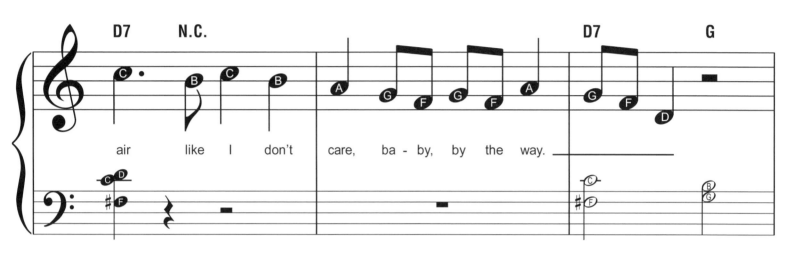

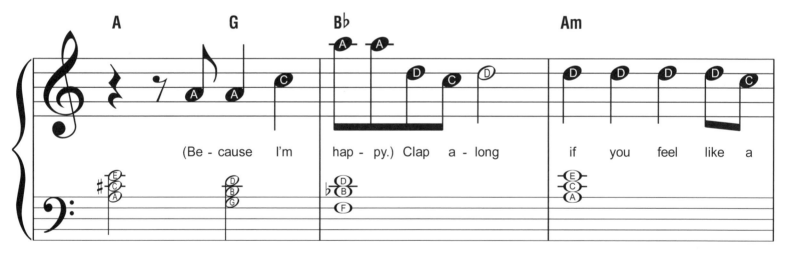

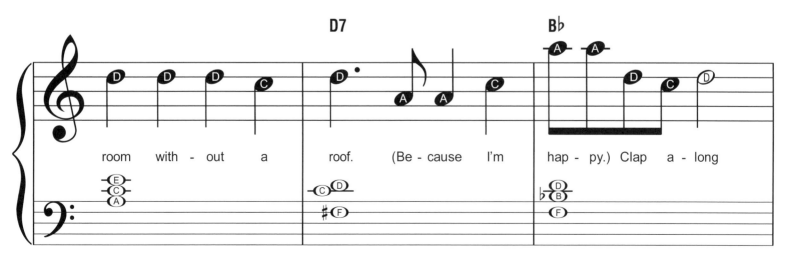

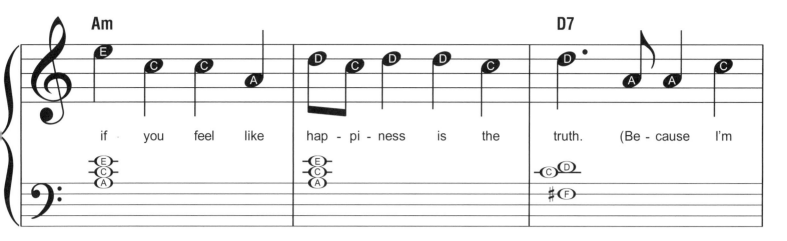

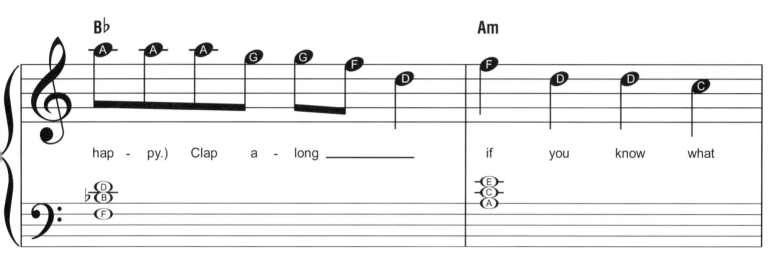

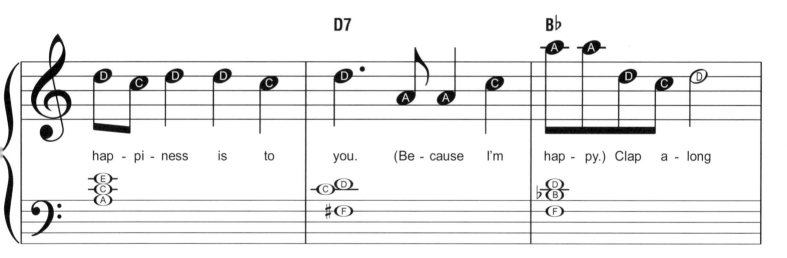

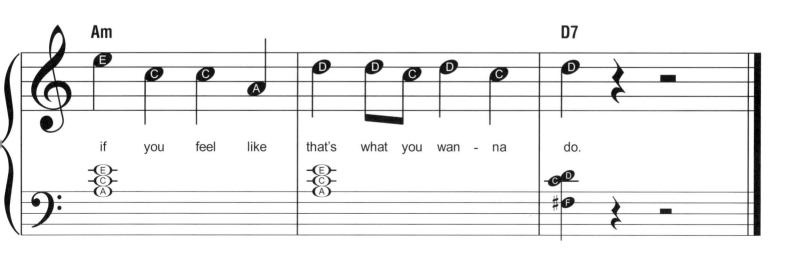

The Middle

Words and Music by Sarah Aarons,
Marcus Lomax, Jordan Johnson,
Anton Zaslavski, Kyle Trewartha,
Michael Trewartha and Stefan Johnson

Let It Go
from FROZEN

Music and Lyrics by Kristen Anderson-Lopez
and Robert Lopez

Flowing

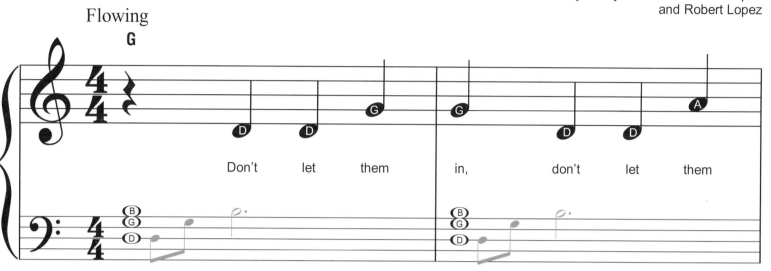

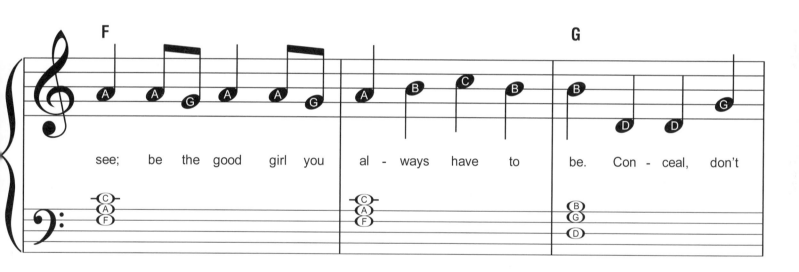

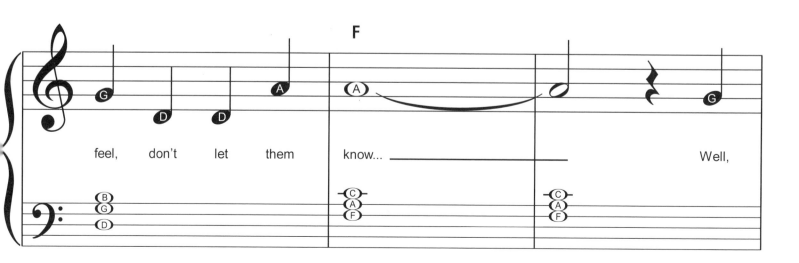

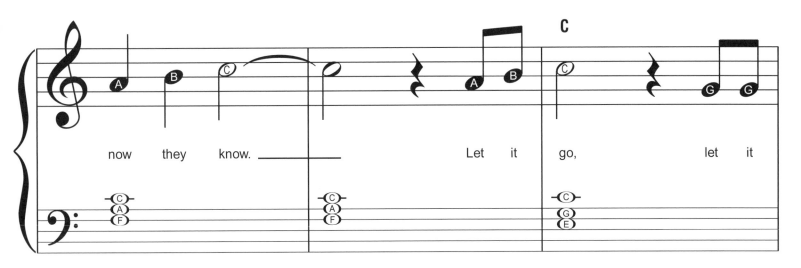

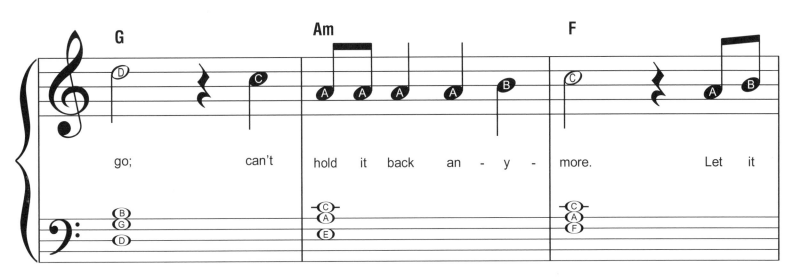

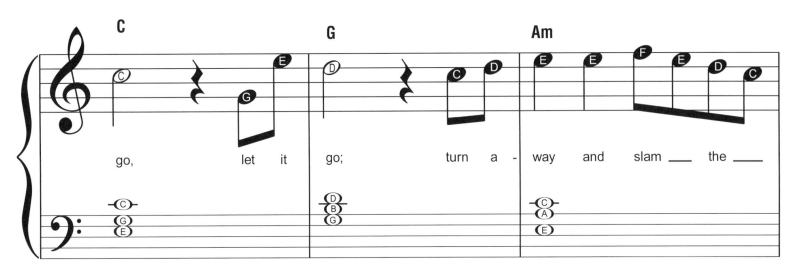

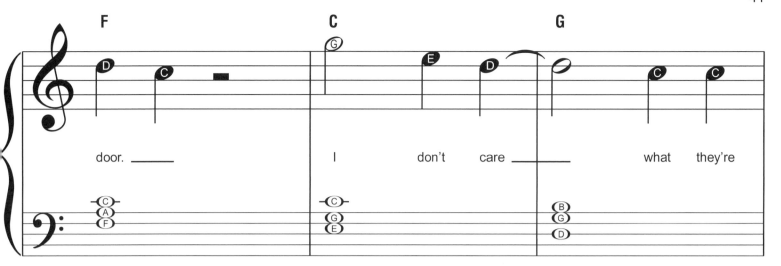

door. _____ I don't care _____ what they're

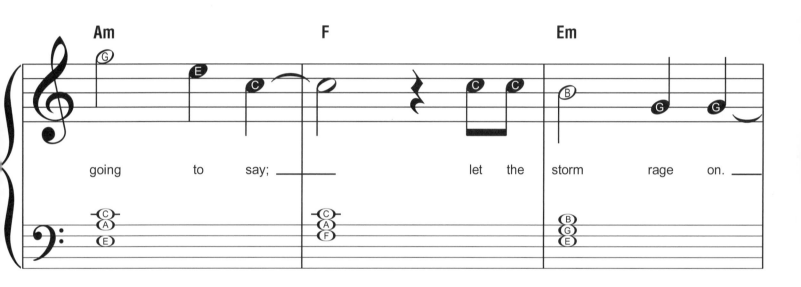

going to say; _____ let the storm rage on. _____

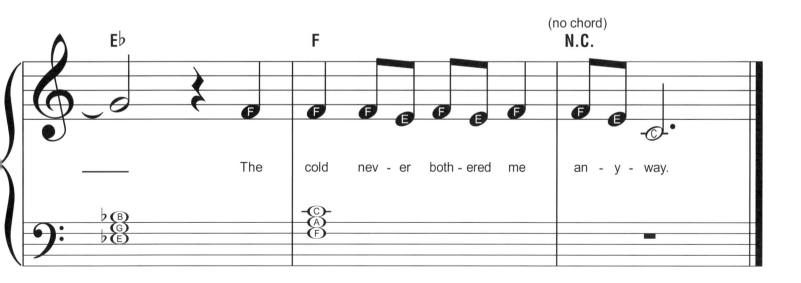

_____ The cold nev - er both - ered me an - y - way.

A Million Dreams
from THE GREATEST SHOWMAN

Words and Music by Benj Pasek
and Justin Paul

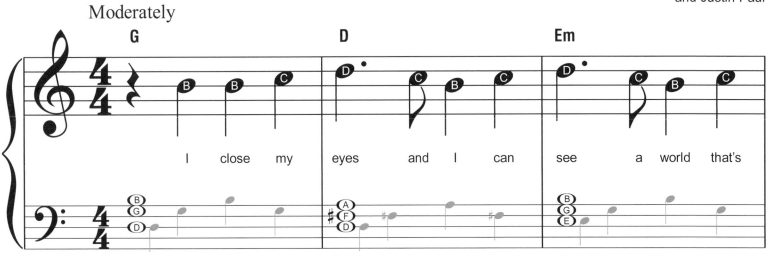

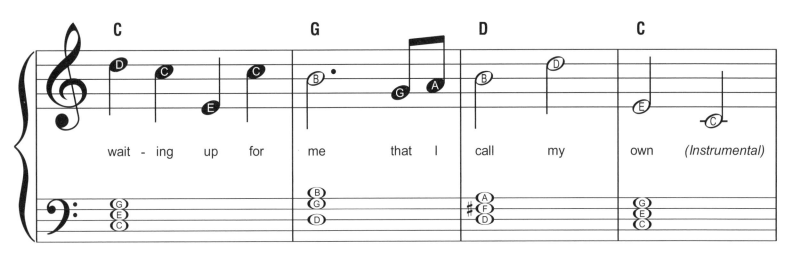

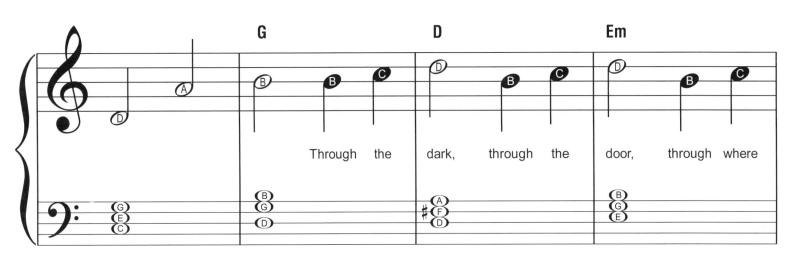

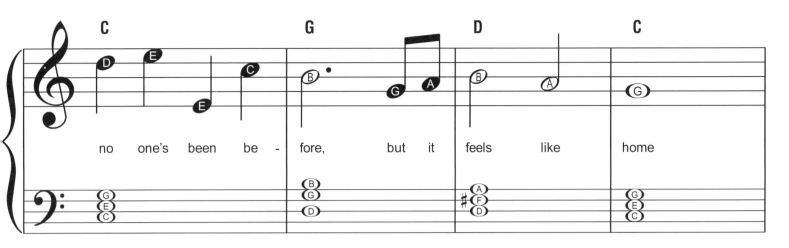

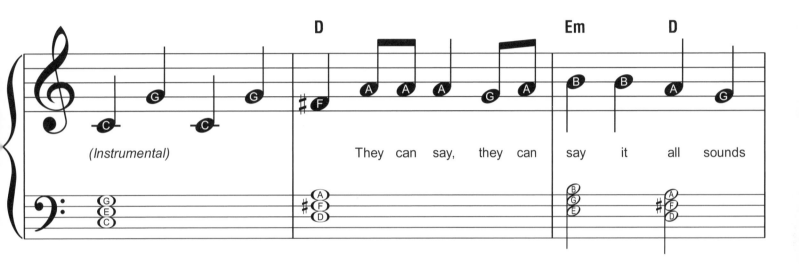

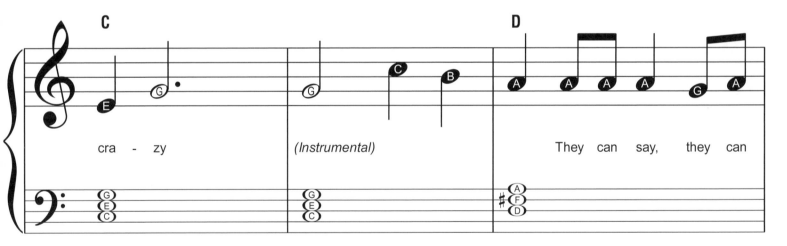

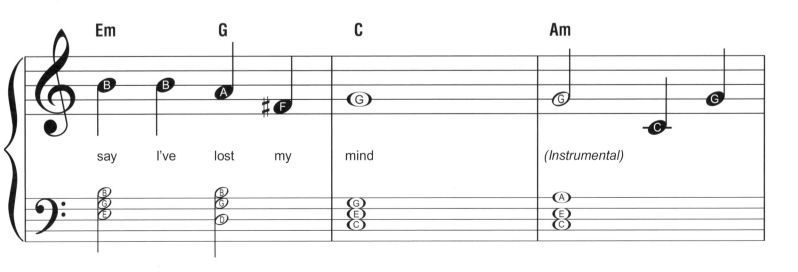

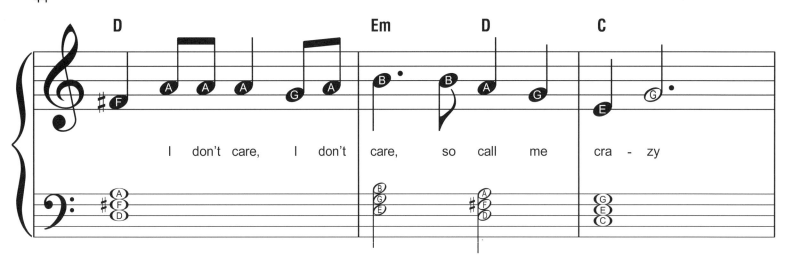

I don't care, I don't care, so call me cra - zy

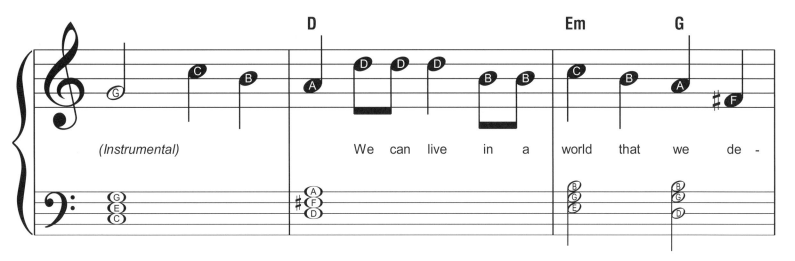

(Instrumental)

We can live in a world that we de -

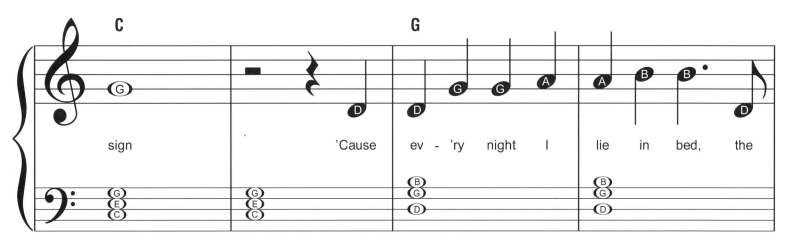

sign 'Cause ev - 'ry night I lie in bed, the

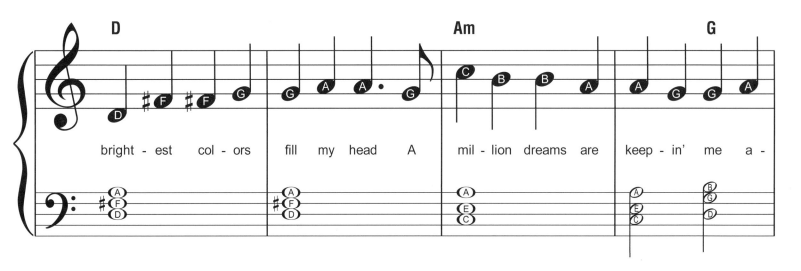

bright - est col - ors fill my head A mil - lion dreams are keep - in' me a -

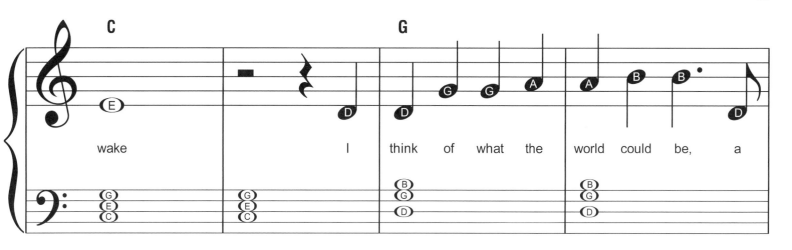

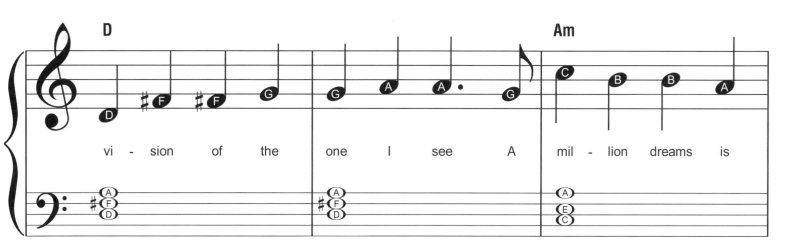

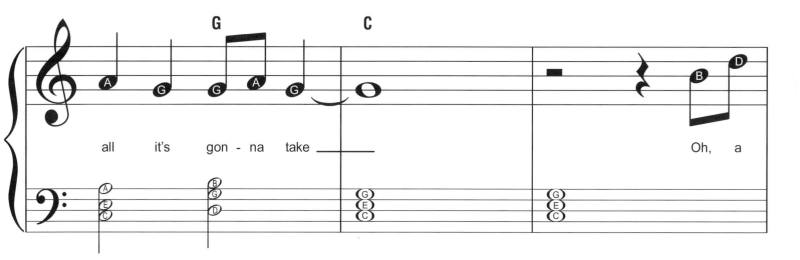

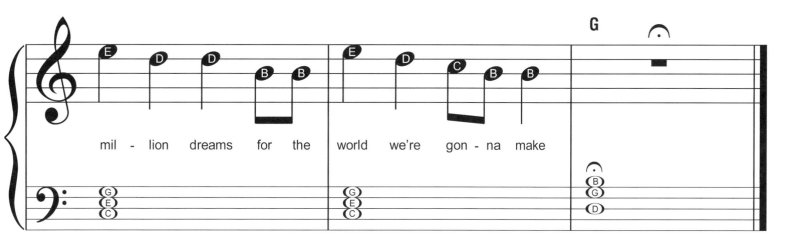

No Tears Left to Cry

Words and Music by Ariana Grande,
Savan Kotecha, Max Martin
and Ilya

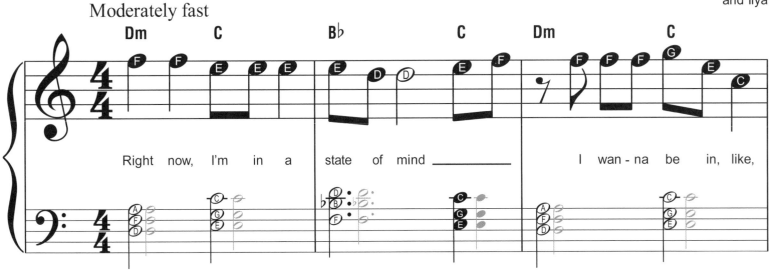

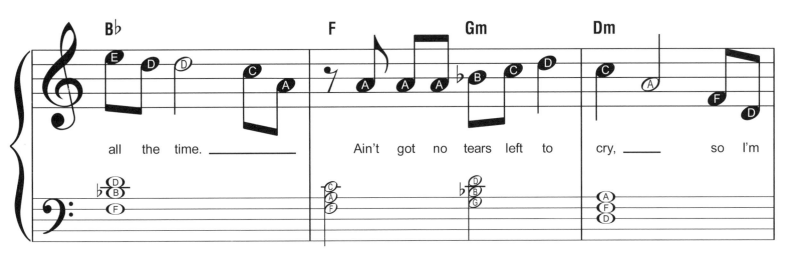

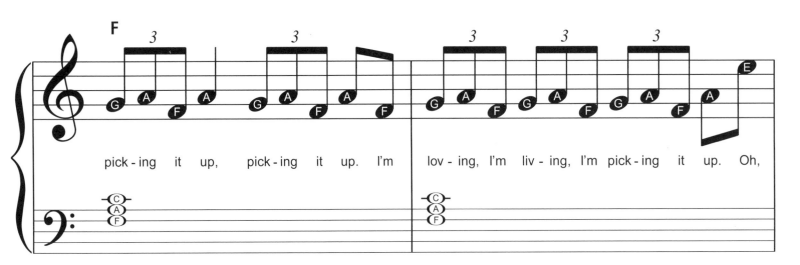

One Call Away

Words and Music by Charlie Puth,
Justin Franks, Breyan Isaac,
Matt Prime, Blake Anthony Carter
and Maureen McDonald

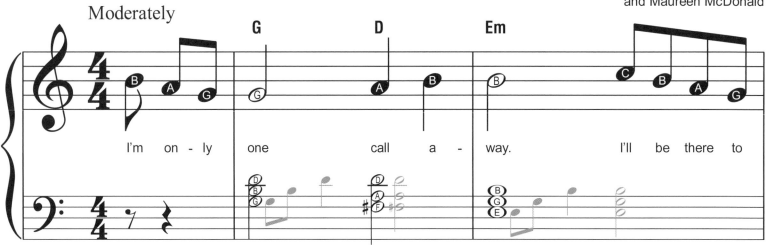

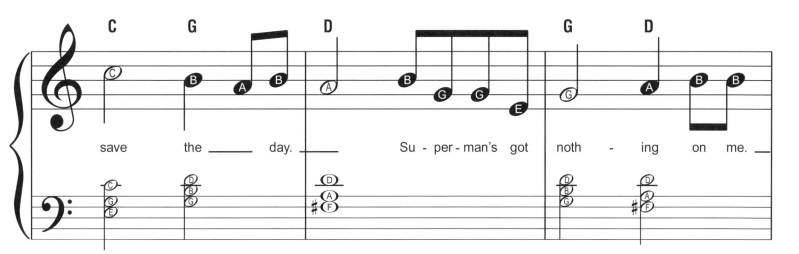

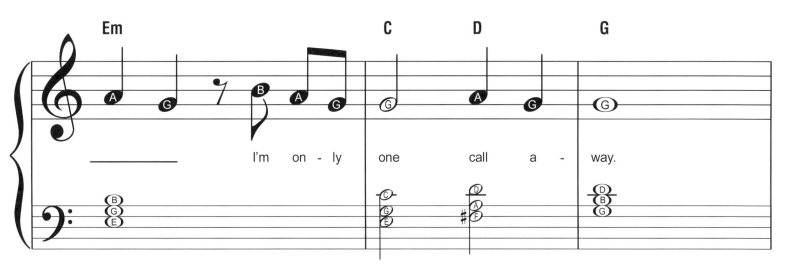

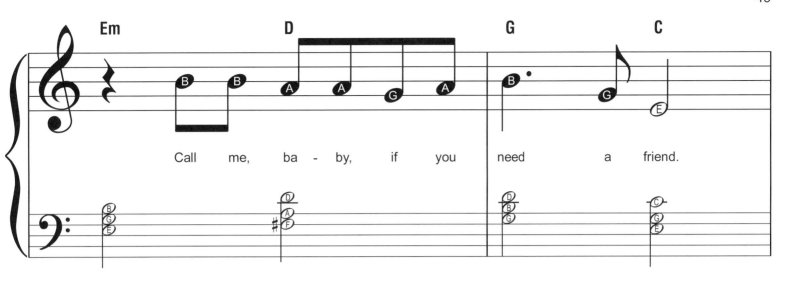

Call me, ba - by, if you need a friend.

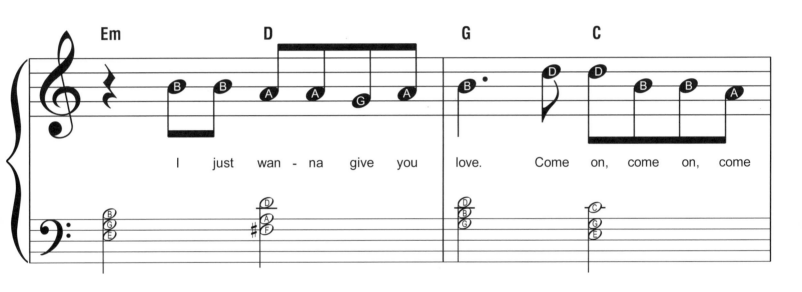

I just wan - na give you love. Come on, come on, come

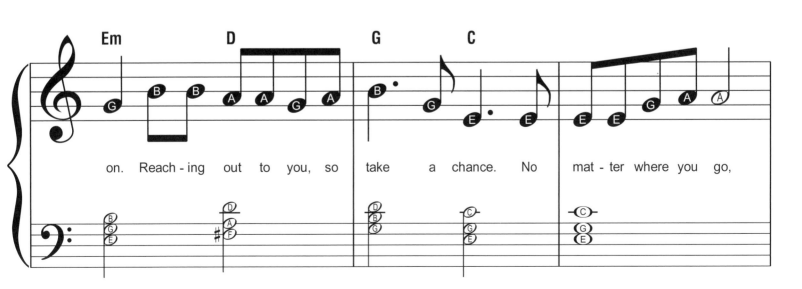

on. Reach - ing out to you, so take a chance. No mat - ter where you go,

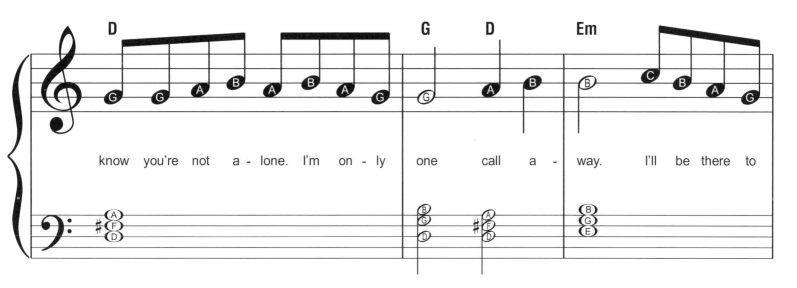

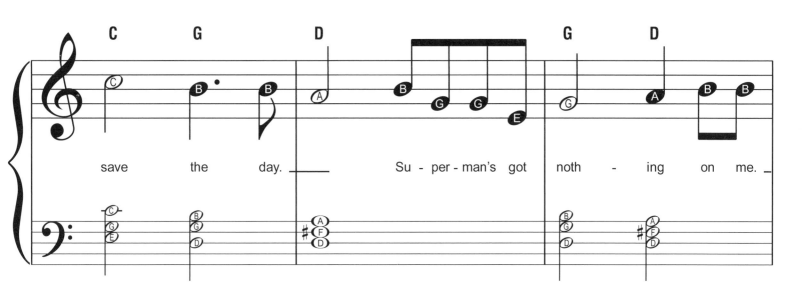

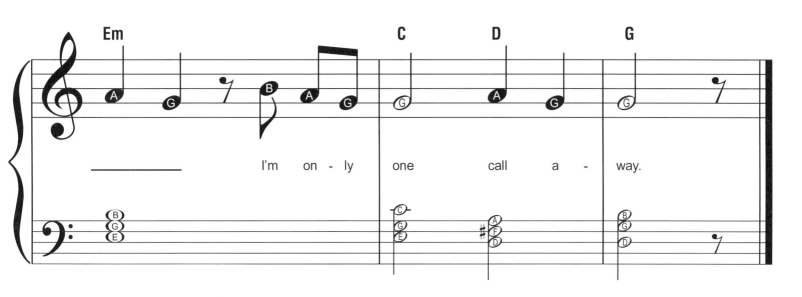

Ocean Eyes

Words and Music by
Finneas O'Connell

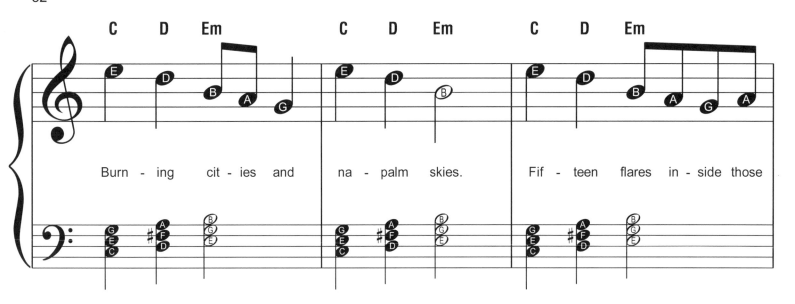

Burn - ing cit - ies and na - palm skies. Fif - teen flares in - side those

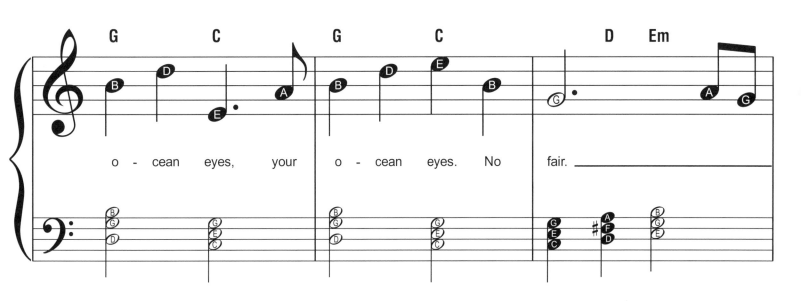

o - cean eyes, your o - cean eyes. No fair. _____

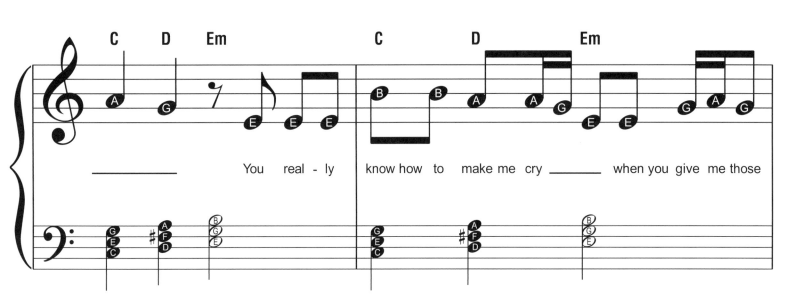

_____ You real - ly know how to make me cry _____ when you give me those

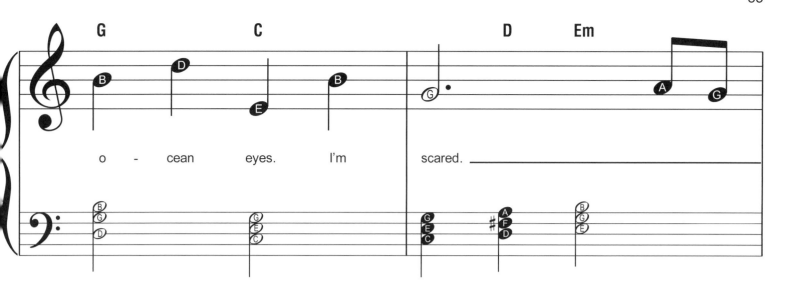

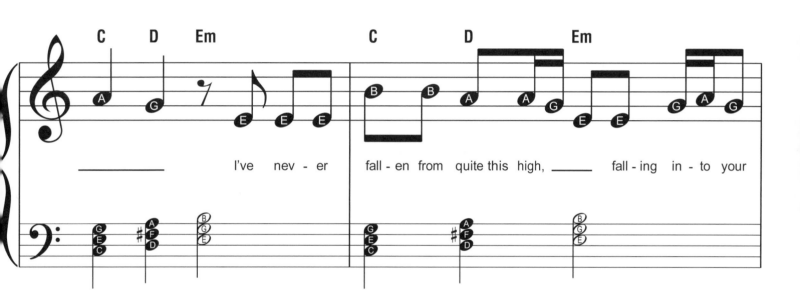

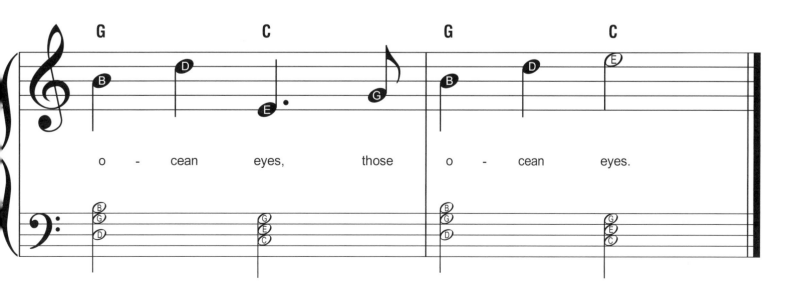

Pompeii

Words and Music by
Dan Smith

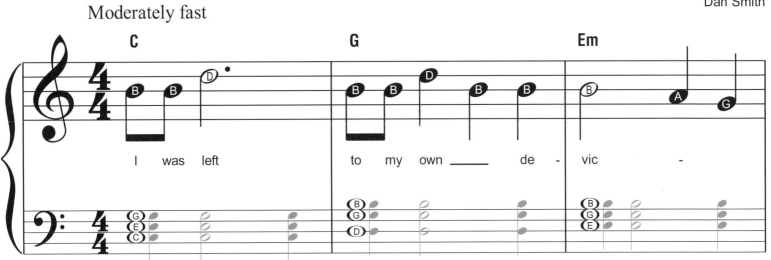

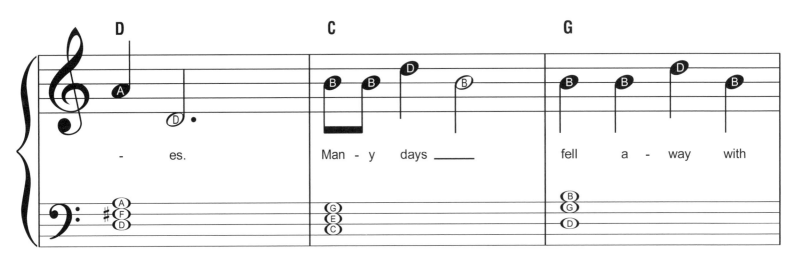

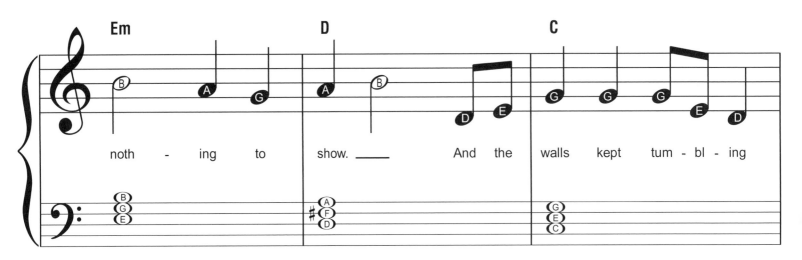

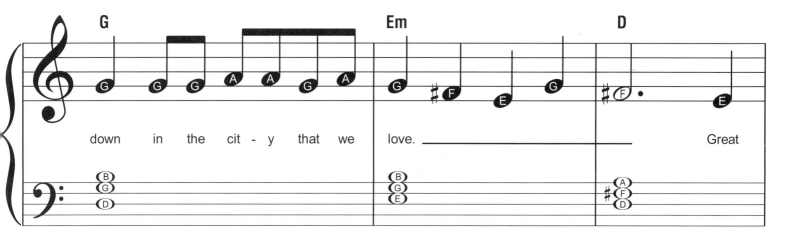

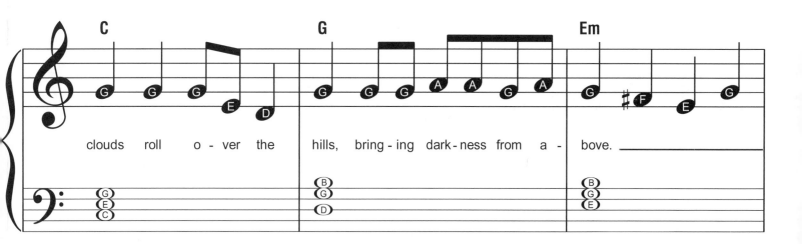

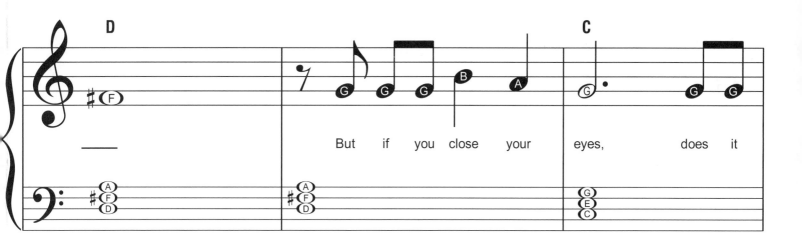

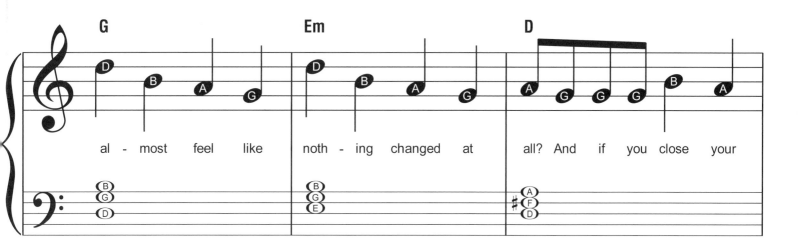

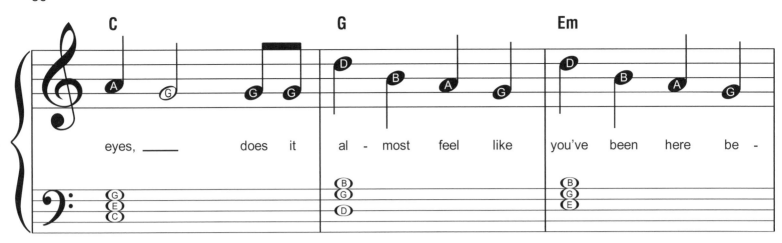

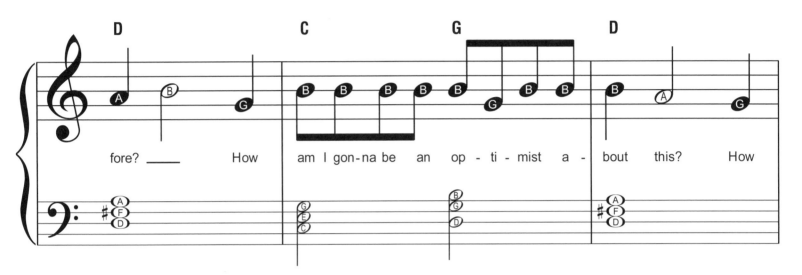

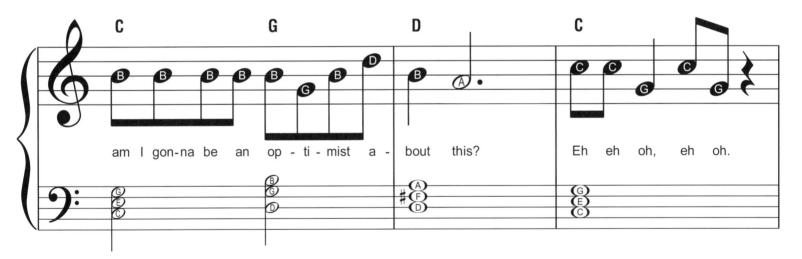

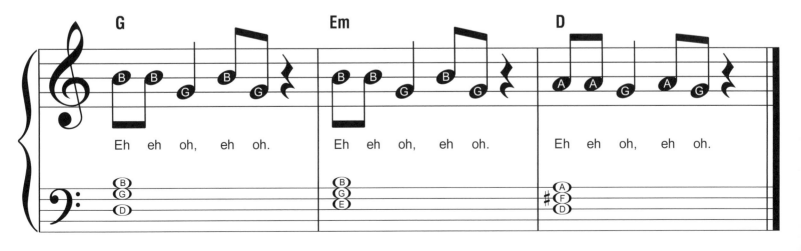

100 Years

Words and Music by
John Ondrasik

Moderately fast

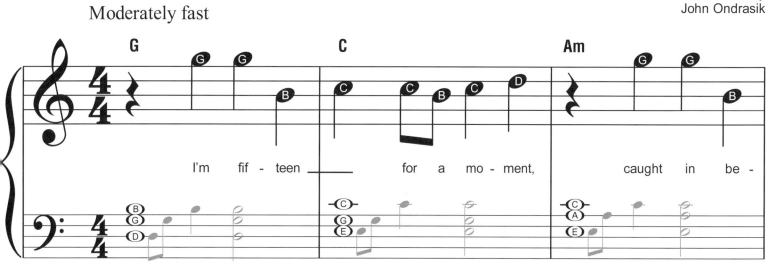

I'm fif - teen ___ for a mo - ment, caught in be -

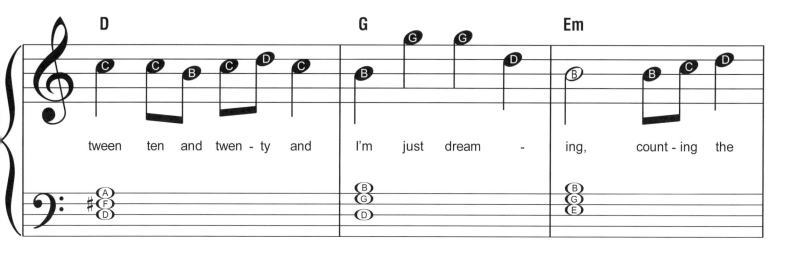

tween ten and twen - ty and I'm just dream - ing, count - ing the

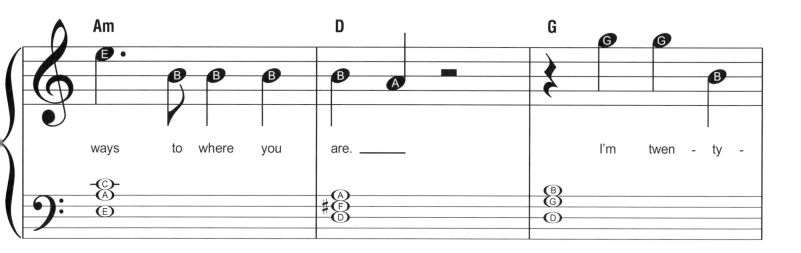

ways to where you are. ___ I'm twen - ty -

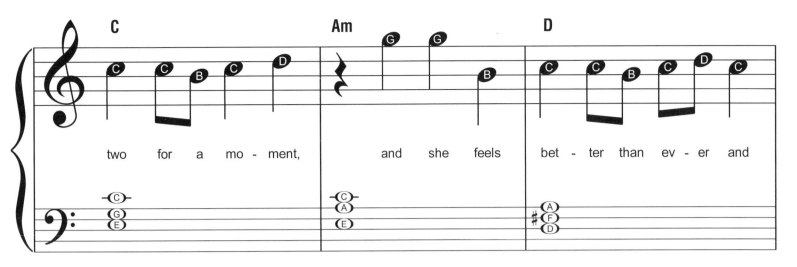

two for a mo - ment, and she feels bet - ter than ev - er and

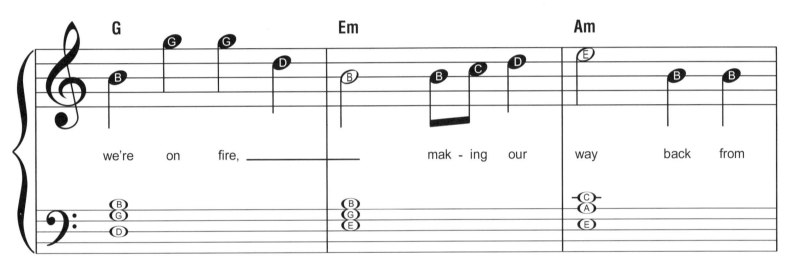

we're on fire, _____ mak - ing our way back from

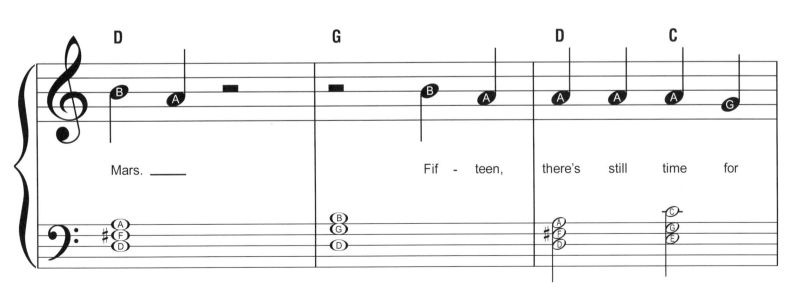

Mars. ___ Fif - teen, there's still time for

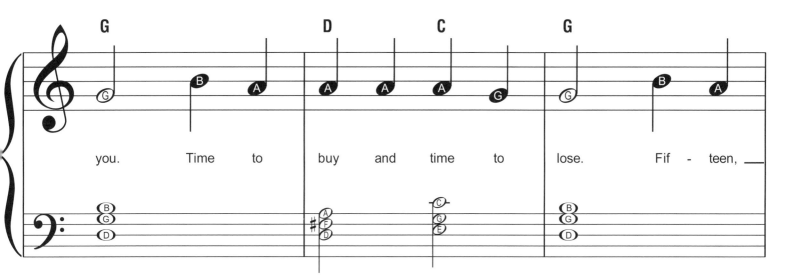

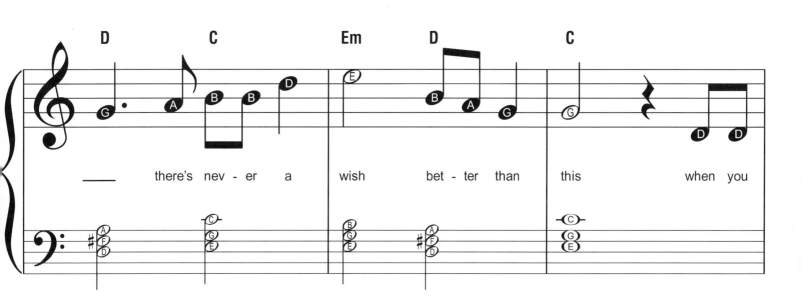

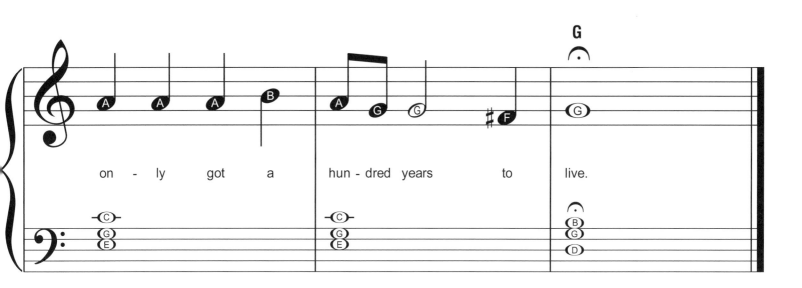

Scars to Your Beautiful

Words and Music by Alessia Caracciolo,
Warren Felder, Coleridge Tillman
and Andrew Wansel

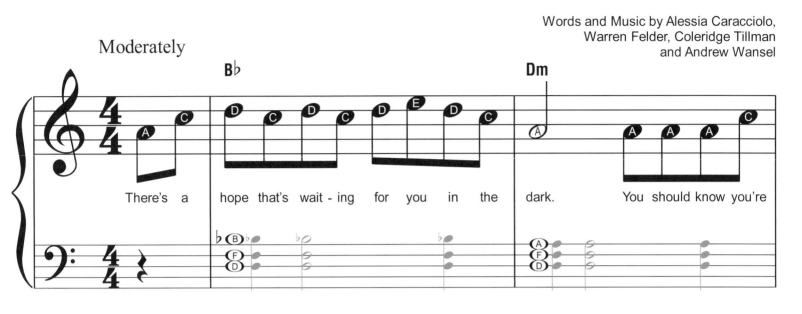

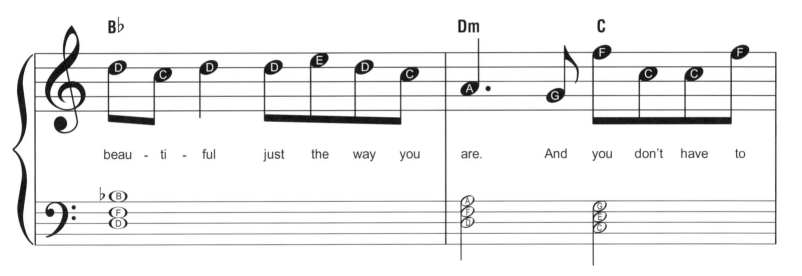

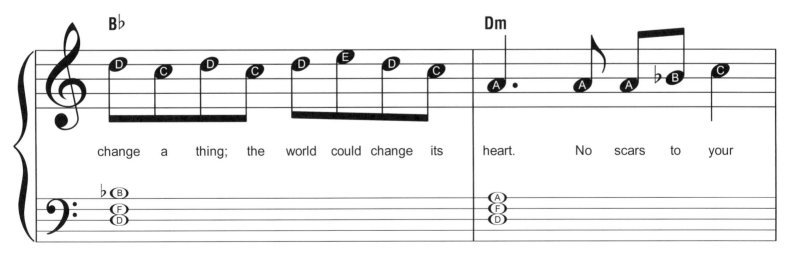

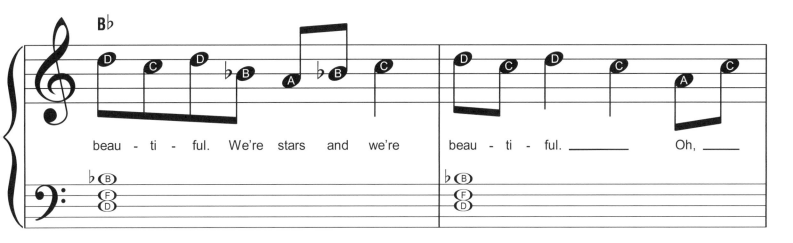

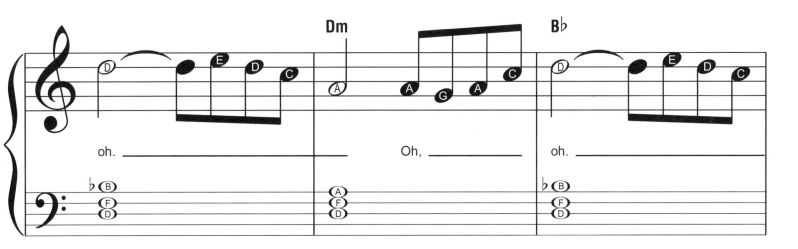

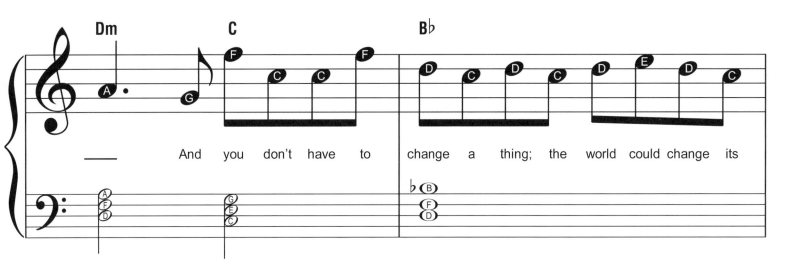

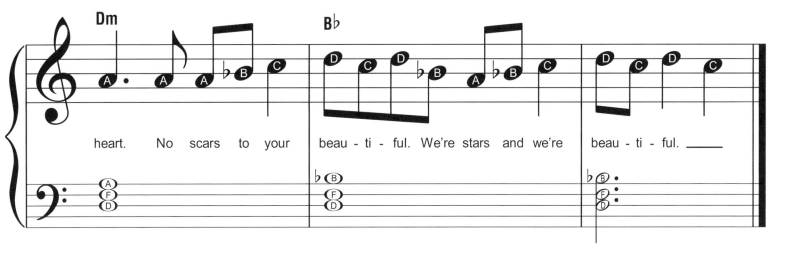

Shake It Off

Words and Music by Taylor Swift,
Max Martin and Shellback

Moderately fast

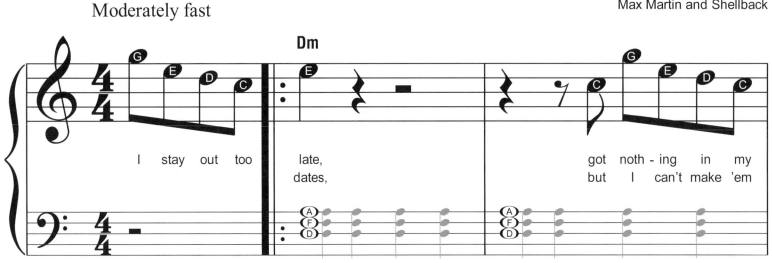

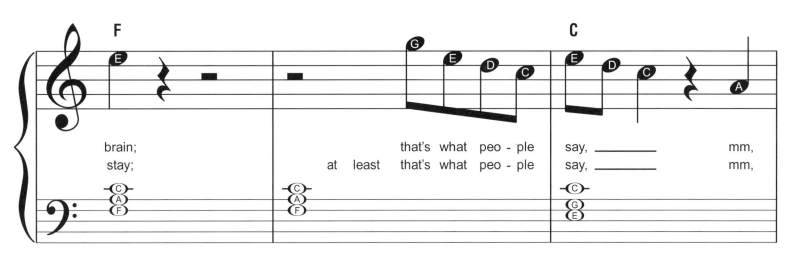

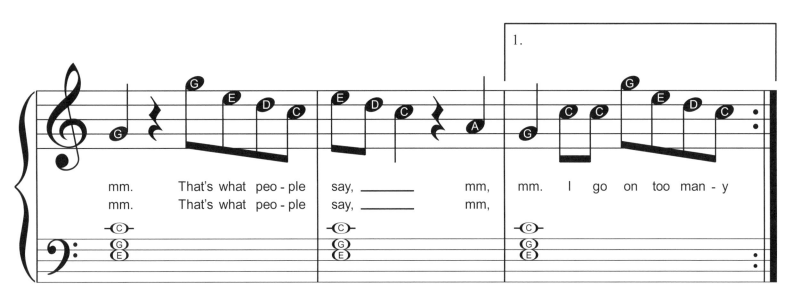

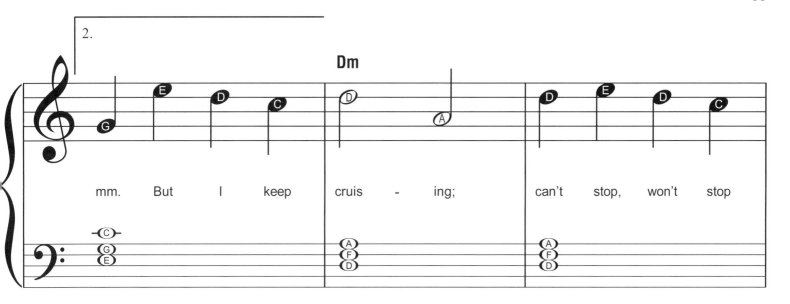

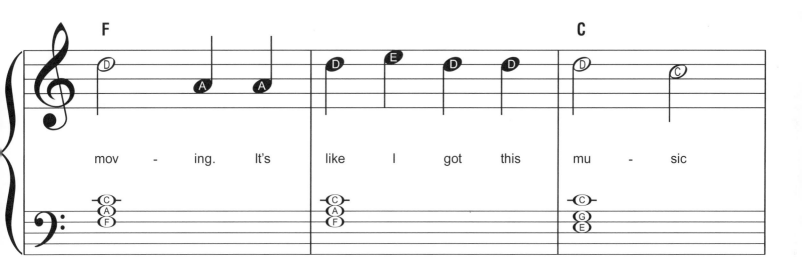

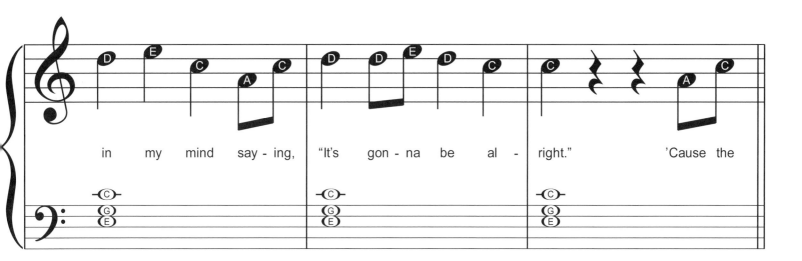

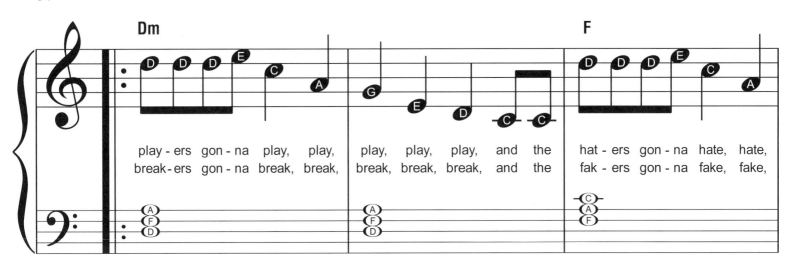

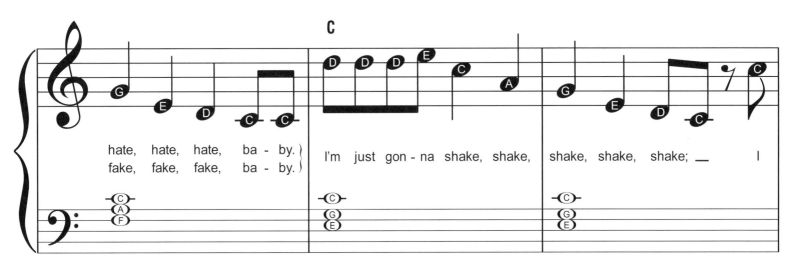

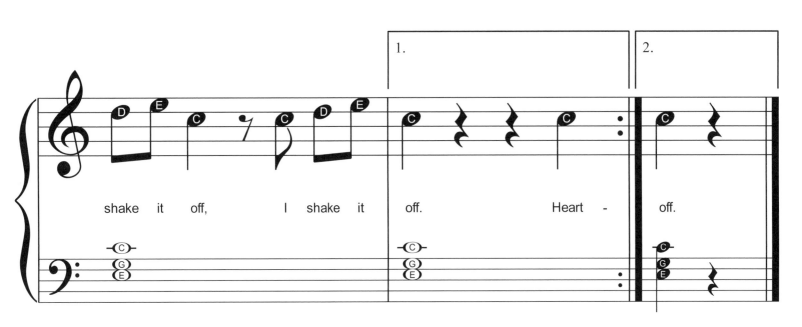

Rude

Words and Music by Nasri Atweh,
Mark Pellizzer, Alex Tanas,
Ben Spivak and Adam Messinger

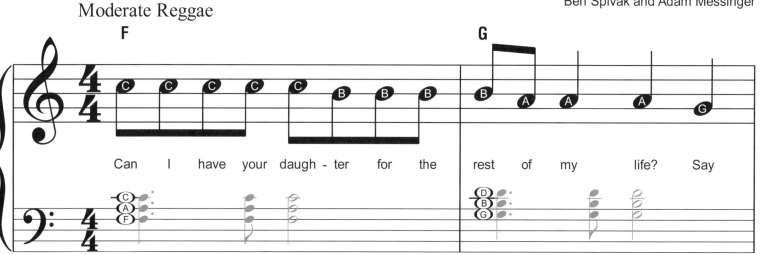

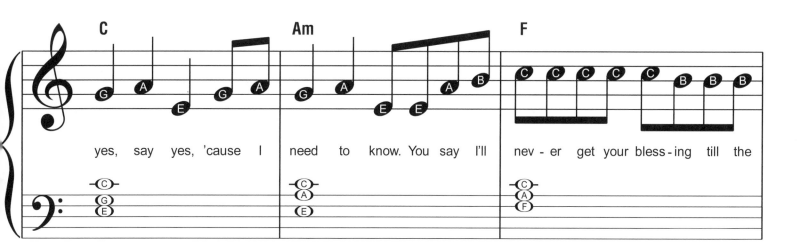

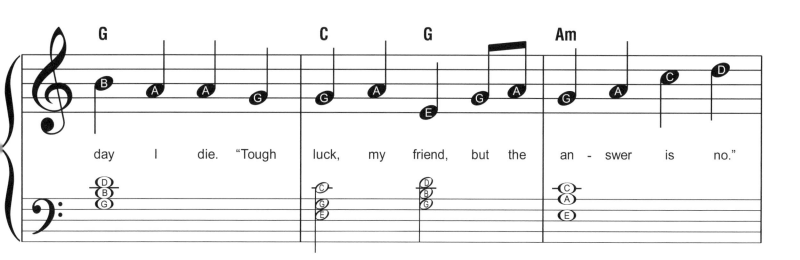

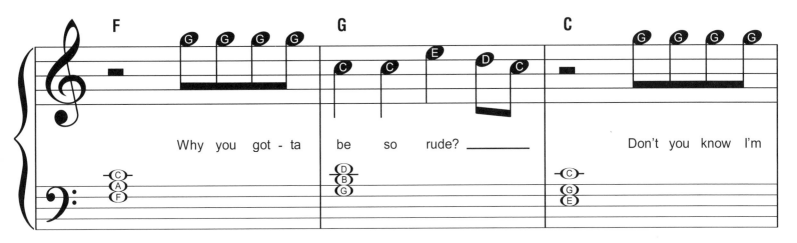

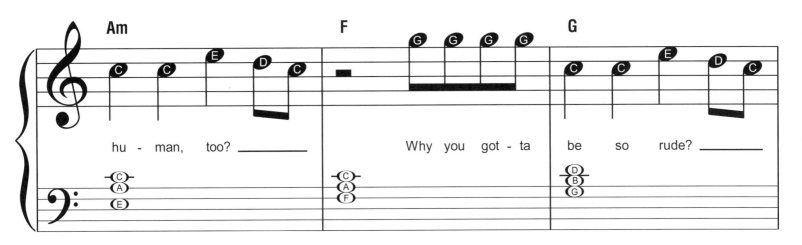

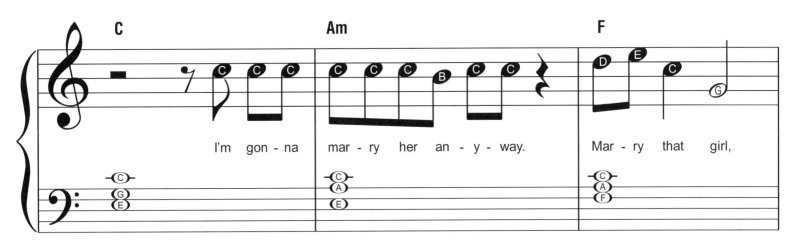

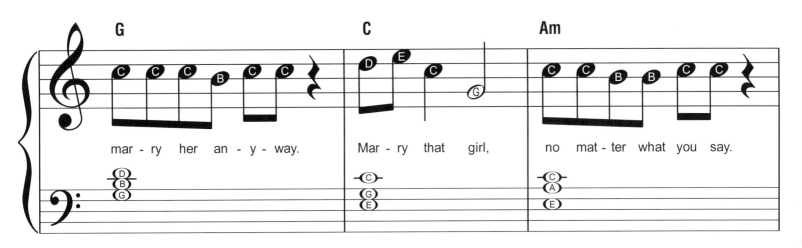

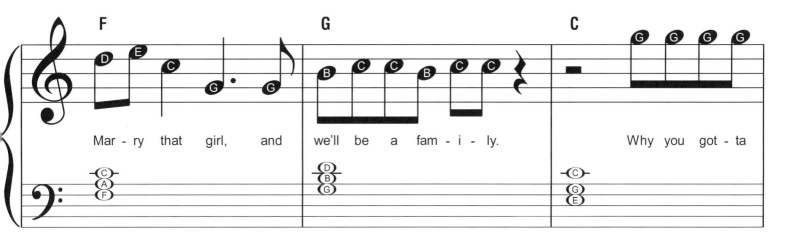

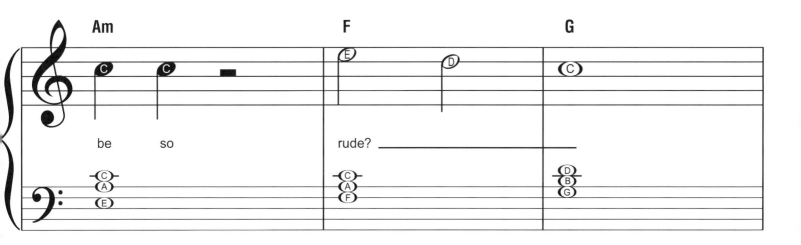

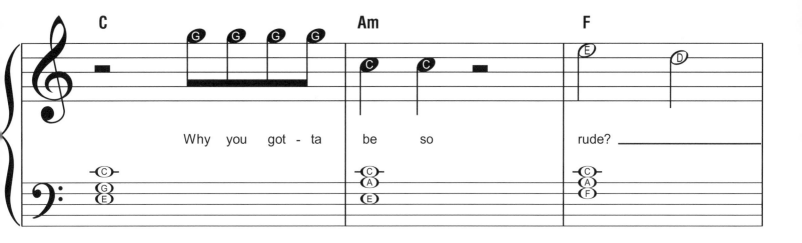

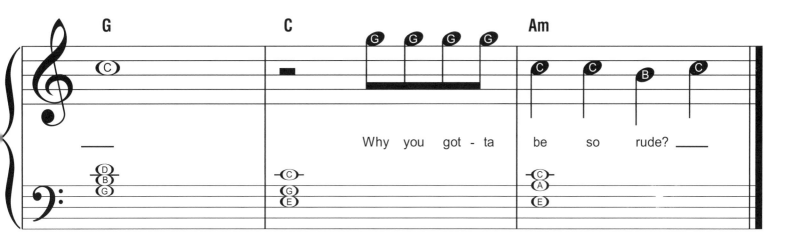

Stressed Out

Words and Music by
Tyler Joseph

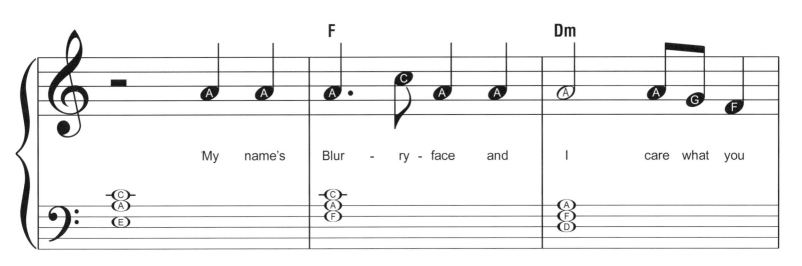

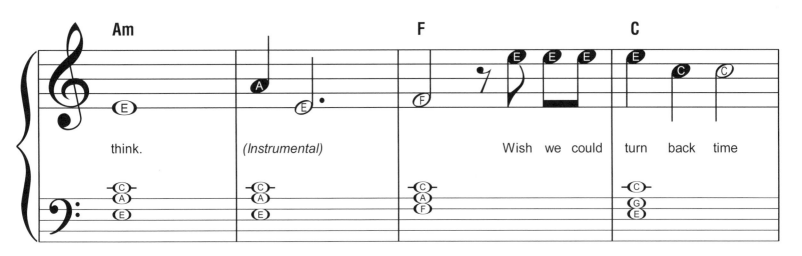

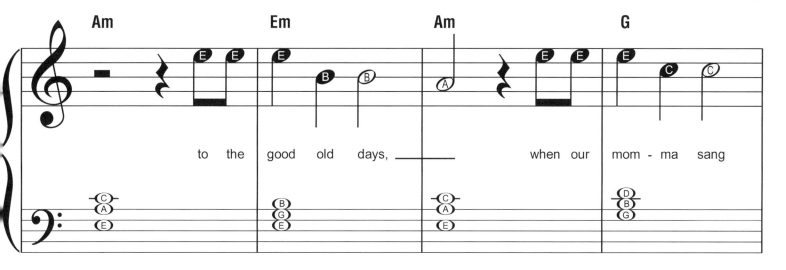

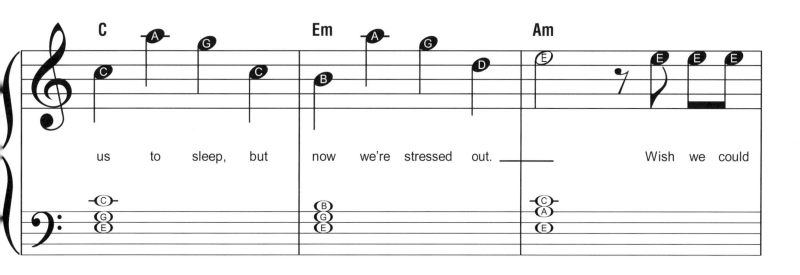

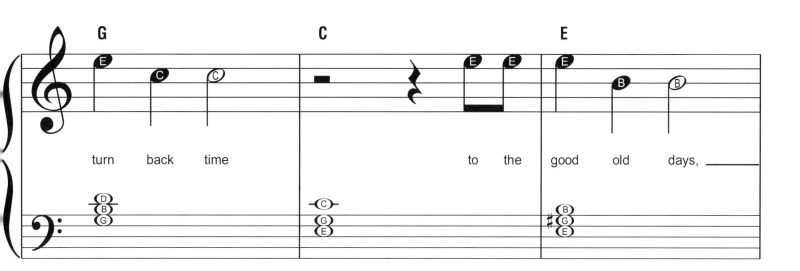

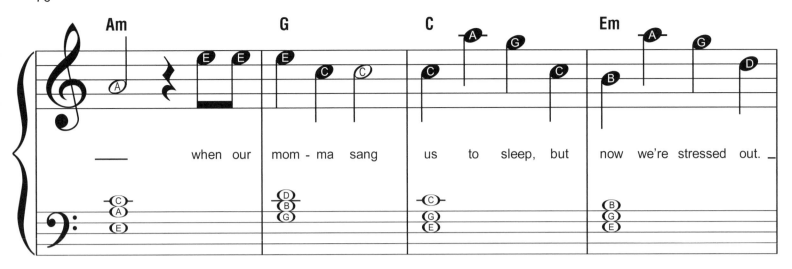

when our mom - ma sang us to sleep, but now we're stressed out. ___

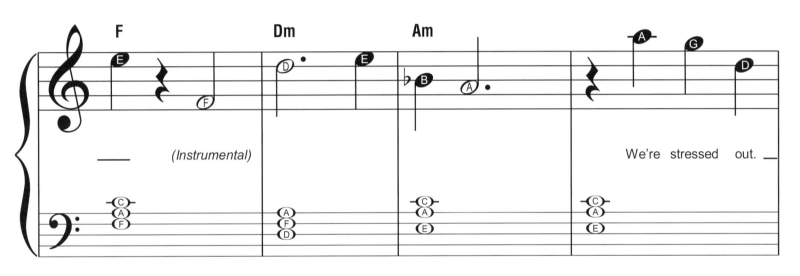

___ *(Instrumental)* We're stressed out.

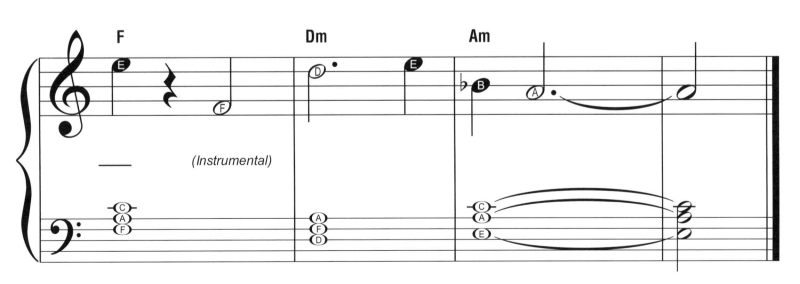

___ *(Instrumental)*

Something Just Like This

Words and Music by Andrew Taggart,
Chris Martin, Guy Berryman,
Jonny Buckland and Will Champion

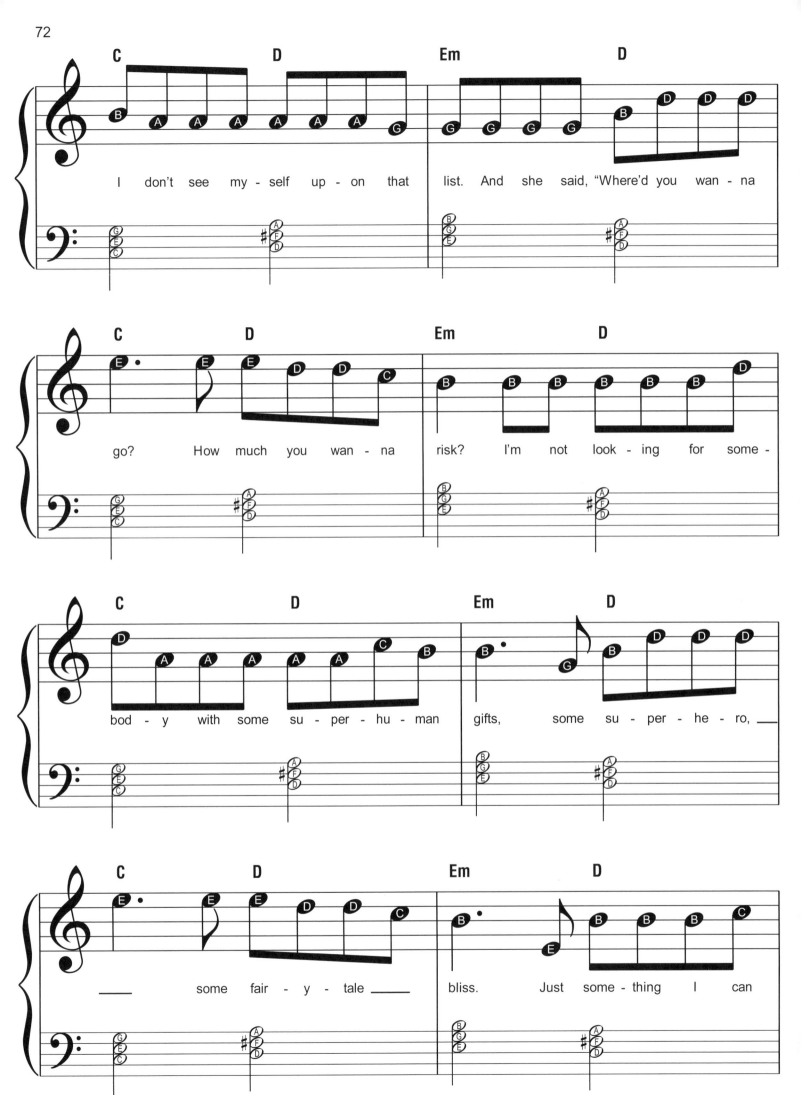

Sunflower
from SPIDER-MAN: INTO THE SPIDER-VERSE

Words and Music by Austin Richard Post,
Carl Austin Rosen, Khalif Brown,
Carter Lang, Louis Bell
and Billy Walsh

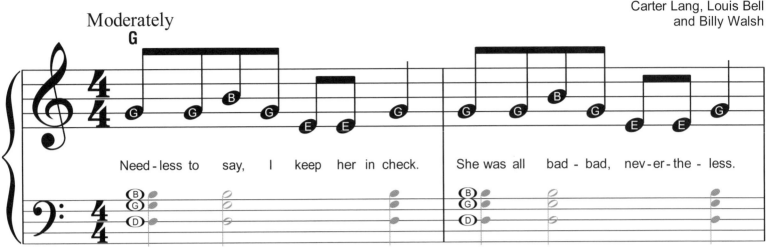

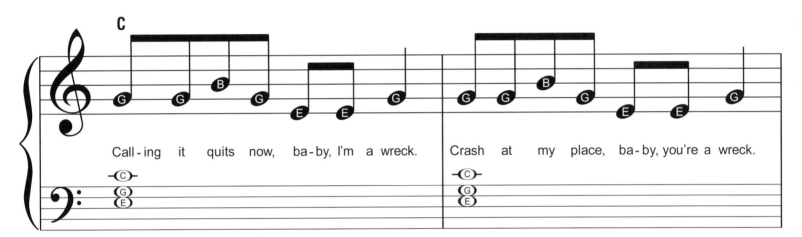

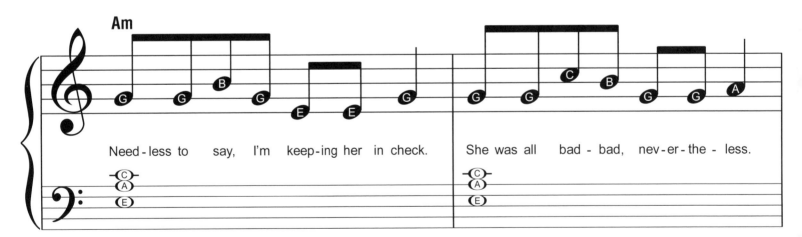

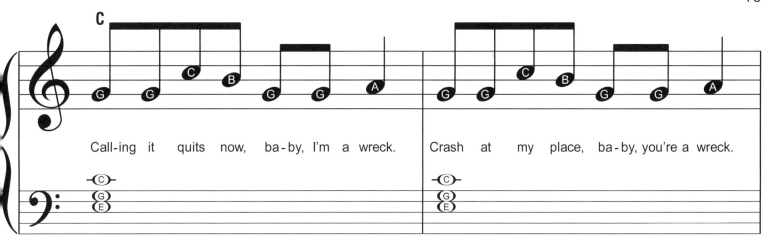

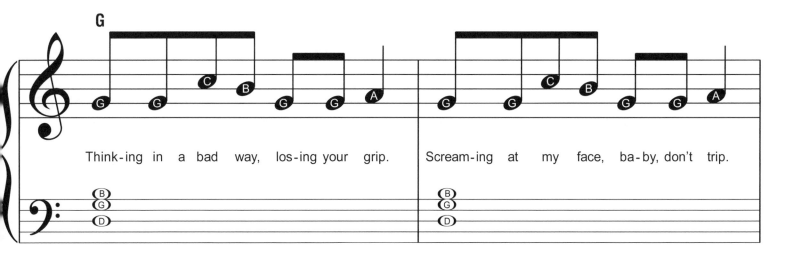

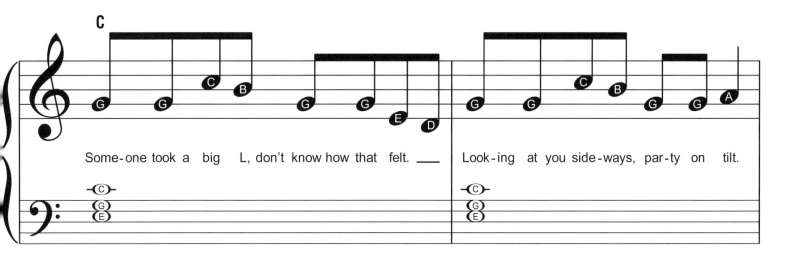

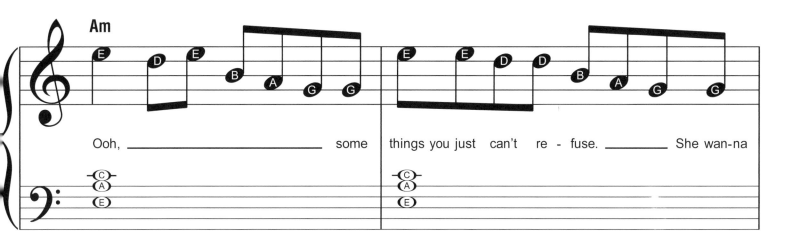

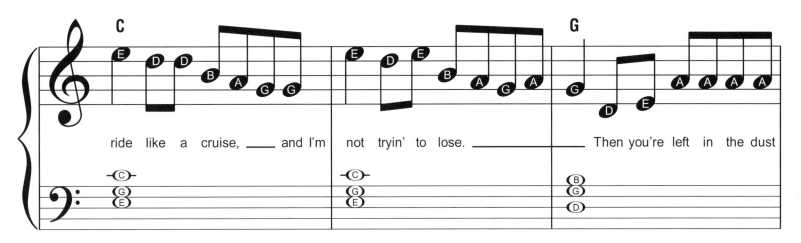

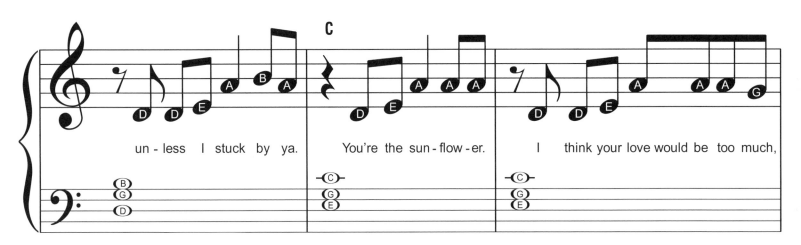

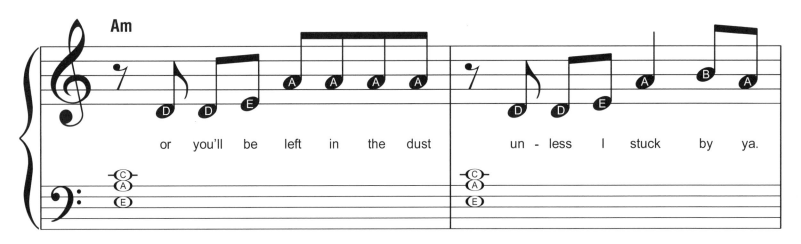

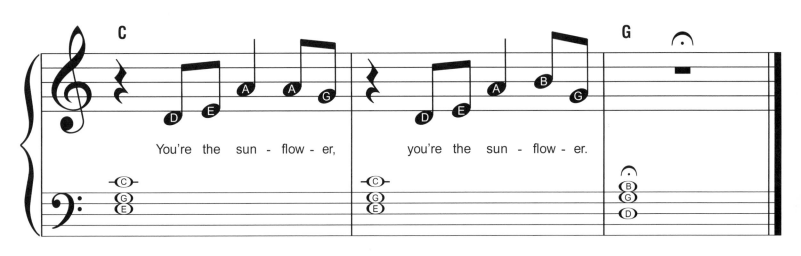

There's Nothing Holdin' Me Back

Words and Music by Shawn Mendes,
Geoffrey Warburton, Teddy Geiger
and Scott Harris

Moderately fast

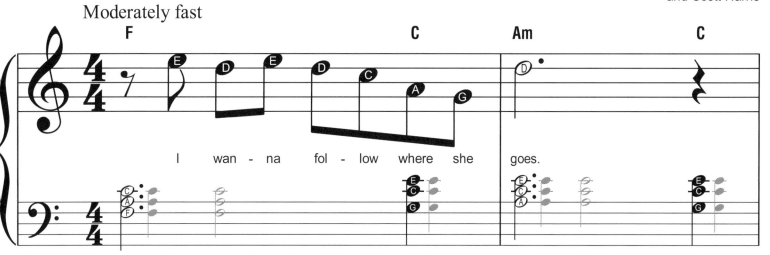

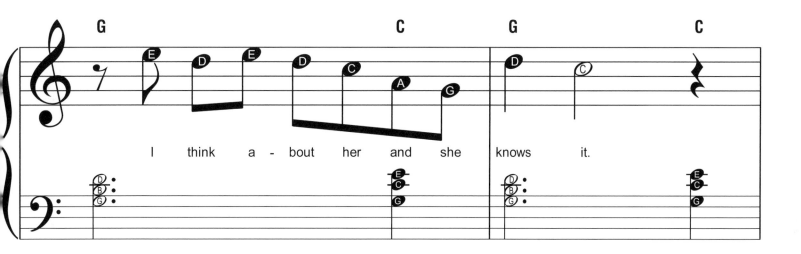

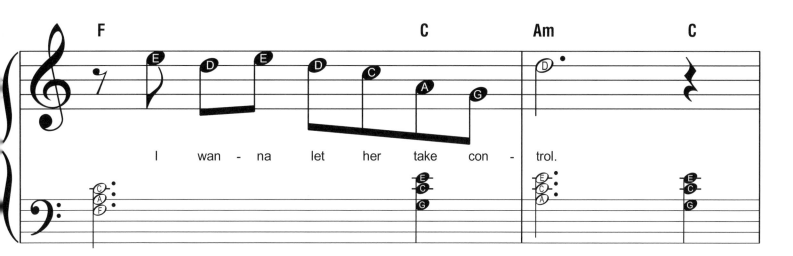

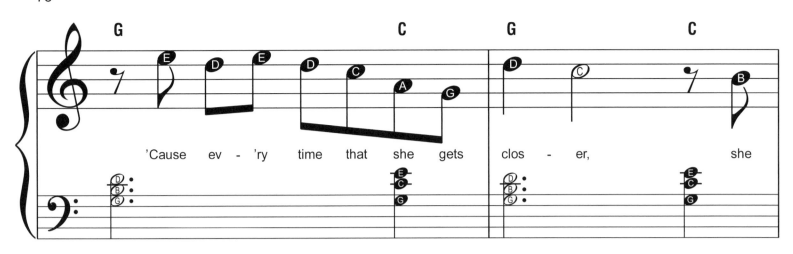

'Cause ev - 'ry time that she gets clos - er, she

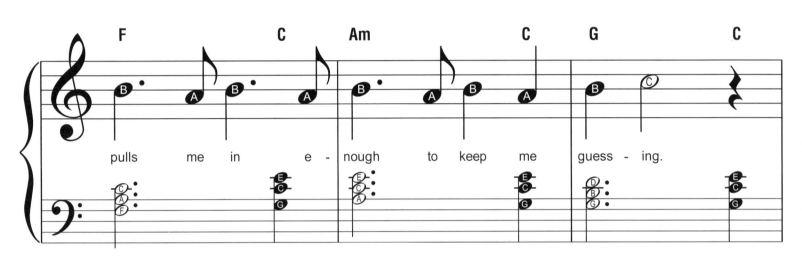

pulls me in e - nough to keep me guess - ing.

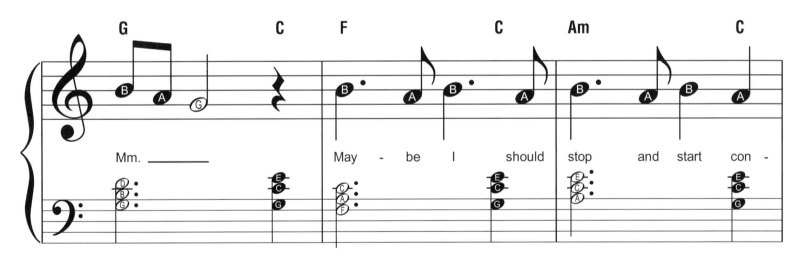

Mm. _____ May - be I should stop and start con -

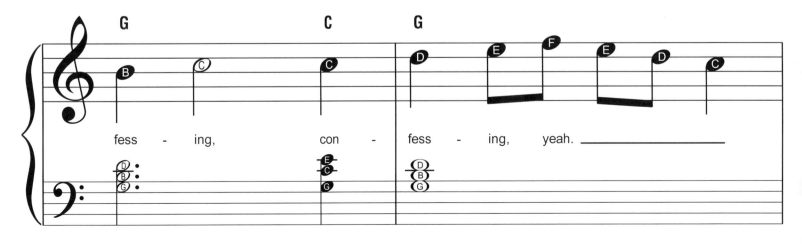

fess - ing, con - fess - ing, yeah. _____

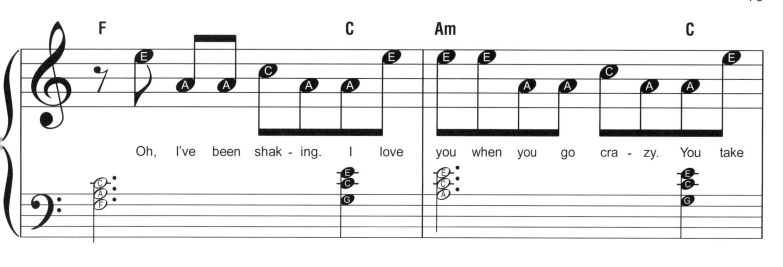

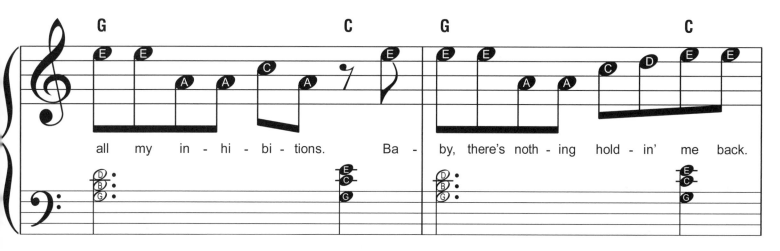

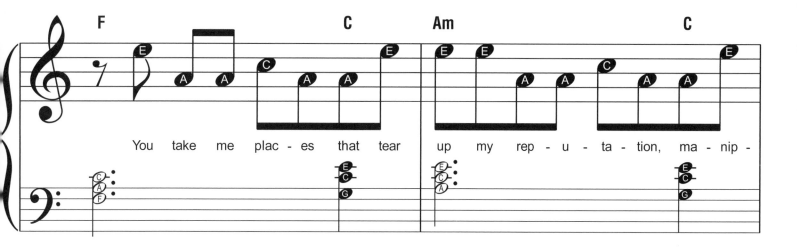

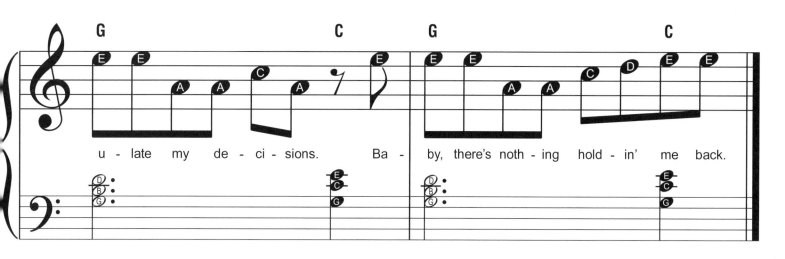

Wake Me Up

Words and Music by Aloe Blacc,
Tim Bergling and Michael Einziger

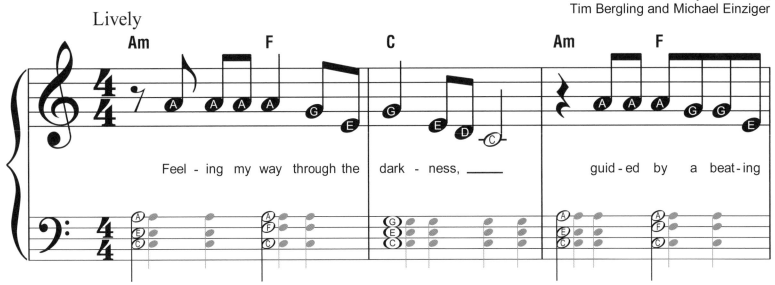

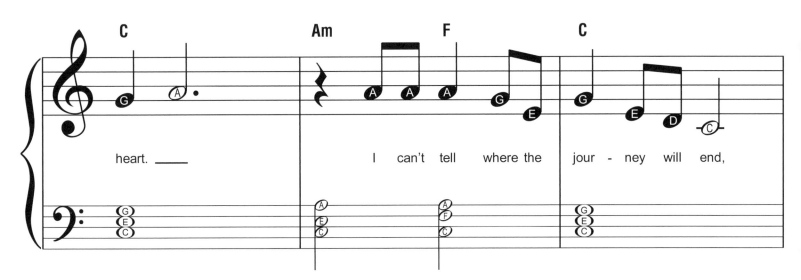

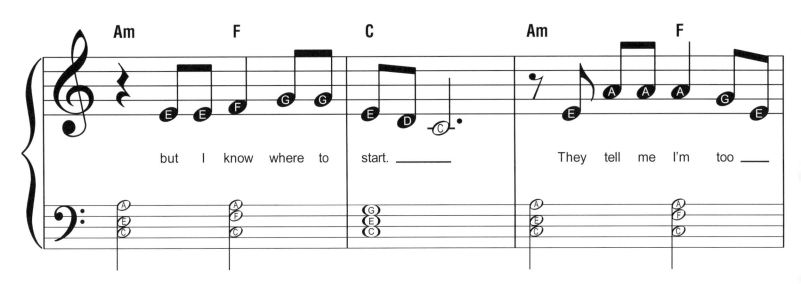

What Makes You Beautiful

Words and Music by Savan Kotecha,
Rami Yacoub and Carl Falk

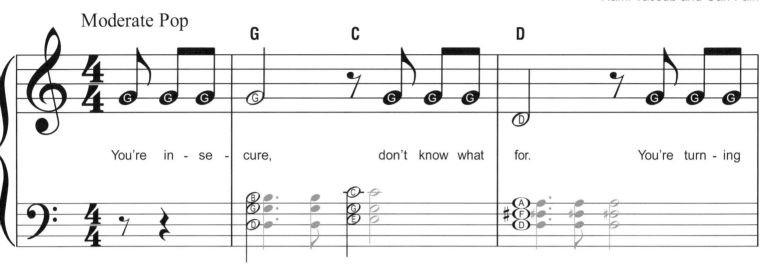

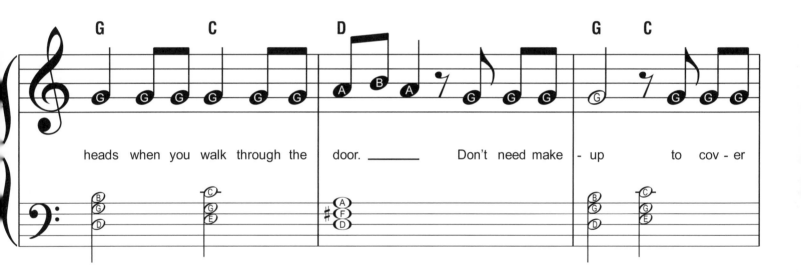

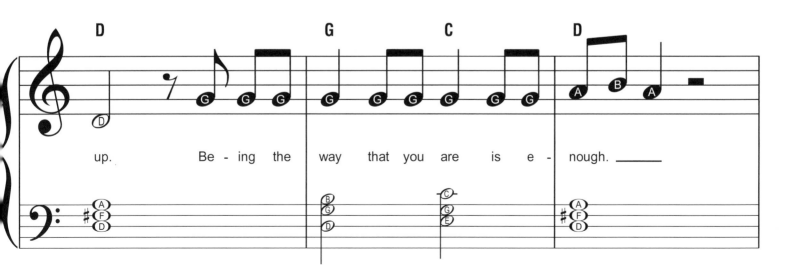

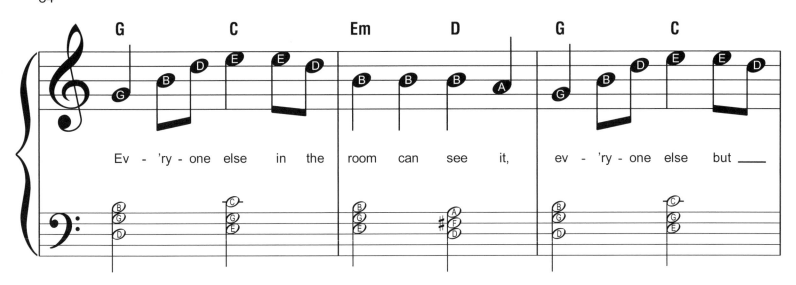

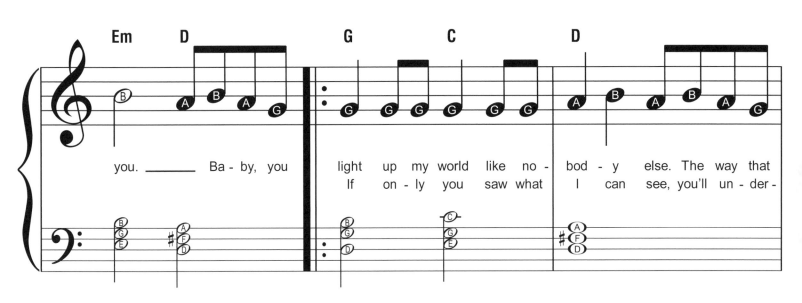

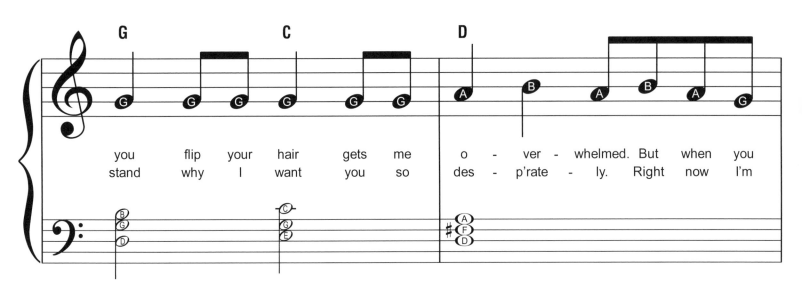

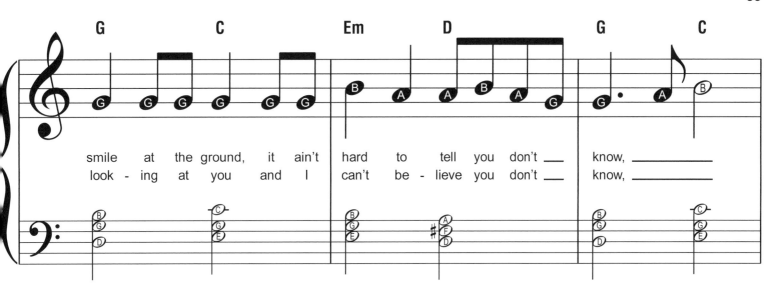

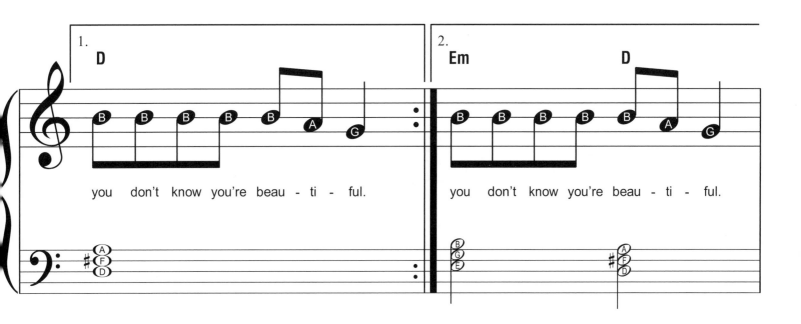

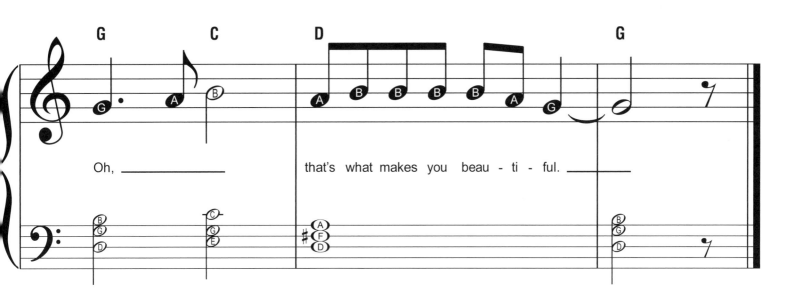

You Can't Stop the Girl

from MALEFICENT: MISTRESS OF EVIL

Words and Music by Bleta Rexha,
Nate Cyphert, Michael Pollack,
Alex Schwartz, Joe Khajadourian,
Sean Nelson, Jeff J. Lin,
Evan Sult and Aaron Huffman

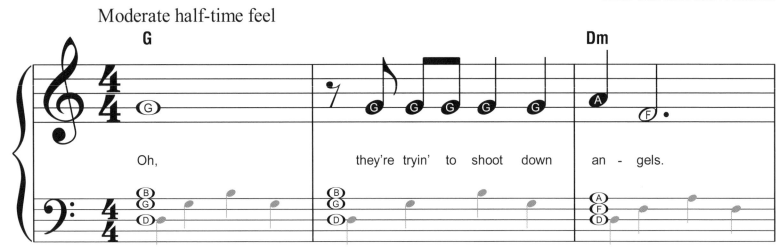

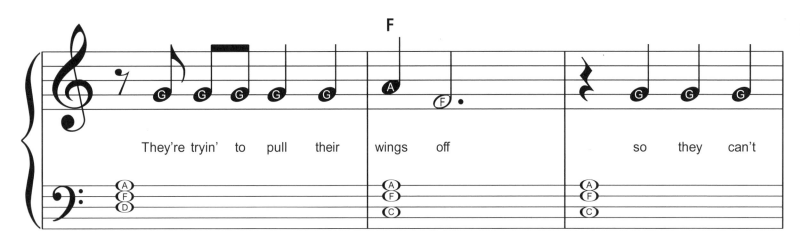

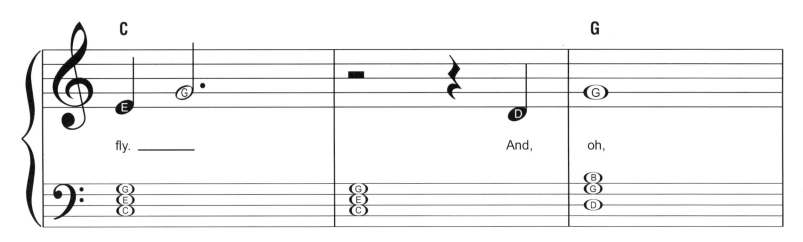

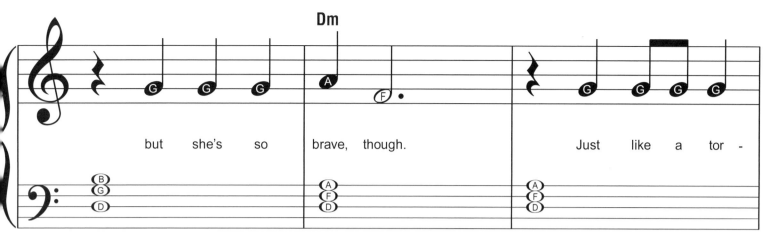

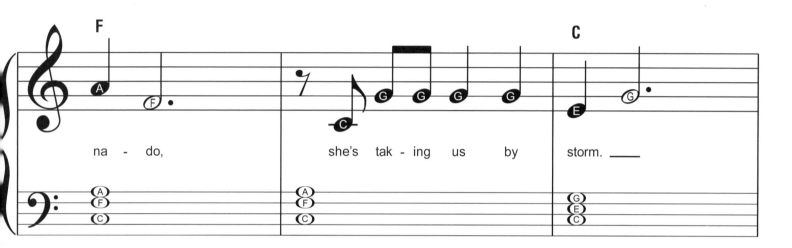

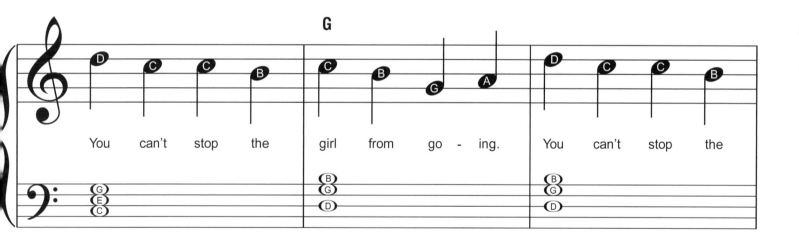

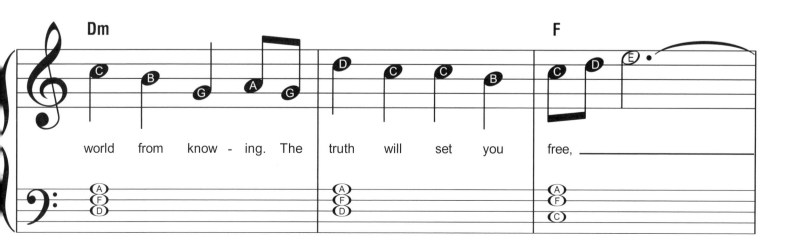

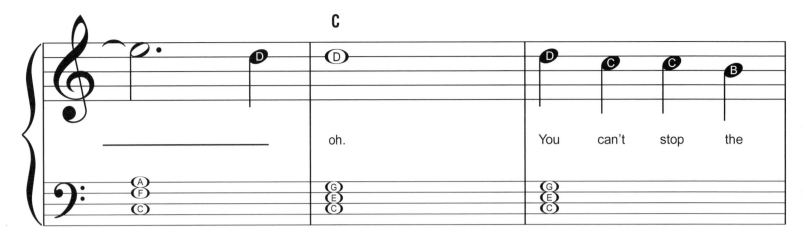

oh.   You can't stop the

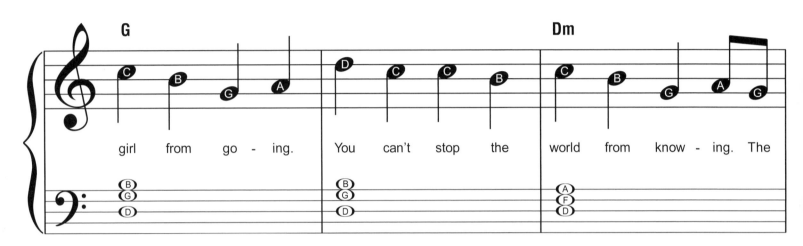

girl from go - ing.   You can't stop the   world from know - ing. The

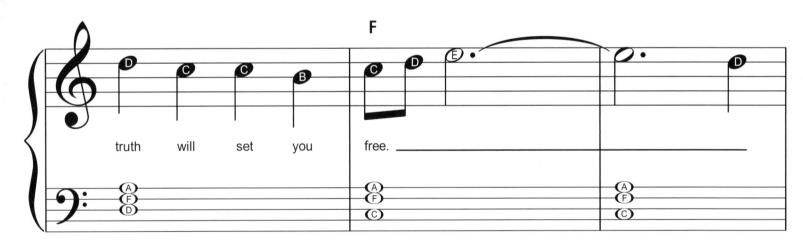

truth will set you   free. _____

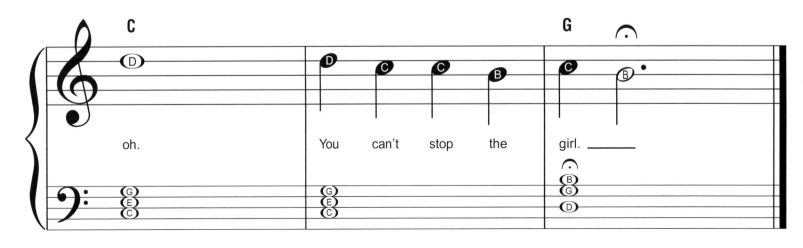

oh.   You can't stop the   girl. _____